Healthcare Designed By Your Body

The Science and Philosophy of BodyTalk – Healthcare Designed By Your Body

By: **Dr. John Veltheim**
Founder of the International BodyTalk Association

Special Thanks to:

Anne Chiang
Certified BodyTalk Practitioner

Amanda Rollefstad
IBA Instructor

Rosilyn Kinnersley
IBA Instructor

Ms. Ellany Whelan
Certified BodyTalk Practitioner

First published in 2013
PaRama LLC
2750 Stickney Point Rd. #203
Sarasota, Florida 34231, USA
First Edition – April 2013

For information regarding permission:
Phone +1.941.921.7443
Fax +1.941.924.3779
Toll Free (US only) 1.877.519.9119
Or contact us on the web at: www.ibaglobalhealing.com
ISBN# 978-1-929762-29-3

Notice to the Reader:

Care has been taken to confirm the accuracy of the information presented in this book. However, the authors, editors, and publisher are not responsible for errors or omissions or for any consequences from application of the information contained herein and make no warranty, express or implied, with respect to the contents of this publication. Practitioners are independent of the IBA; they are supposed to practice in accordance with their own state and country laws and govern their own operations and regulations.

BodyTalk texts, videos, websites, other printed materials and sessions are designed to promote relaxation and communication within and between various areas of the body. BodyTalk application methods are in no way deemed substitutes for medical diagnoses, treatments and/or medications and should not be interpreted as such. IN CASE OF A MEDICAL EMERGENCY SEEK APPROPRIATE EMERGENCY CARE.

By following the instructions contained herein, the reader willingly assumes all risks in connection with such instructions. The authors, editors, and publisher make no representations or warranties of any kind, nor are any such representations implied. The authors, editors, and publisher shall not be liable for any special, consequential, or exemplary damages resulting in whole or part, from the reader's use of or reliance upon the material contained herein.

BODYTALK PRINTED MATERIALS, PROGRAMS, LECTURES AND OTHER PRESENTATIONS ARE DESIGNED TO PROVIDE A NON-INVASIVE MODALITY AND SHOULD NOT BE RELIED UPON FOR THE DIAGNOSIS OR TREATMENT OF MENTAL OR PHYSICAL ILLNESSES. THE BODYTALK PRACTITIONER DOES NOT DIAGNOSE DISEASE NOR DOES HE/SHE PERFORM MASSAGE/MANIPULATIONS. THE BODYTALK PRACTITIONER DOES NOT PROVIDE INJECTIONS NOR DOES HE/SHE PRESCRIBE DIETS, HERBS, SUPPLEMENTS OR MEDICATIONS.

*"This book is dedicated to my children,
Sheridan, Anja, Kassie-Maree, and Christopher,
who had to sacrifice valuable "growing up" time
with me so I could develop this system."*

– Dr. John Veltheim

About the Author

John Veltheim is the founder of The BodyTalk System™ and co-founder of both the International BodyTalk Association and International BodyTalk Foundation, which helps fund research and offers BodyTalk Access to people in places where healthcare is not readily available.

He is formally trained as a chiropractor and acupuncturist and served as the former Principal of the Brisbane College of Acupuncture and Natural Therapies for 5 years. Dr. Veltheim's extensive post-graduate studies include applied kinesiology and Bio-energetic therapy. He has also studied osteopathy and sports medicine.

His other areas of expertise include counseling, comparative philosophy, and theology. John also has extensive knowledge in the field of quantum physics and Consciousness and has spent much time lecturing internationally on these topics.

Dr. Veltheim has written numerous magazine and journal articles on The BodyTalk System™ and in his other fields of expertise. Recently, Dr Veltheim's work was published in the Journal of Alternative Medicine Research. The journal's publishers were so impressed with John's development of BodyTalk, that they dedicated an entire volume solely to articles on The BodyTalk System™.

He is the published author of several books including books about Reiki, acupuncture and BodyTalk. He created The BodyTalk System™ course work and developed the PaRama BodyTalk program where quantum physics meets healing at the highest level.

Table of Contents

Foreword

by James Oschman Ph.D.

Quantum BodyTalk: Who is talking, who is listening and how does it work?

The current challenges facing humanity, together with remarkable new opportunities, have led many to contemplate the future of our culture: where are we headed and what are the long-term prospects for the health, survival, and prosperity of humanity?

The idea of daily and dramatic advances in medicine is embedded in our culture, with the news media continually telling us about astounding new drugs and medical technologies. The dramatic advances I will refer to here have little to do with these well-advertised aspects of biomedicine. Instead they relate to the completely non-invasive hands-on and energetic approaches to health. Taken together, these methods have been termed complementary and alternative medicine (CAM), integrative or whole-person medicine. They form the fastest-growing branches of medicine and their popularity with the healthcare consumer is soaring. BodyTalk is a leader in this emerging field as witnessed by the rapid growth in the number of practitioners and, more importantly, by the enthusiasm of these individuals and their clients because of astonishing accomplishments in resolving a wide variety of health issues. Good news travels very fast and BodyTalk has a lot of good news to share, as you will from reading this book.

As a scientist looking at BodyTalk, I note one thing that stands out. A few years ago it was often said that there was no scientific basis for CAM or whole-person medicine or energy medicine, and one can still sometimes hear such statements. When a prominent authority declares that something is impossible, it is always important to look at the origins of the statement. For every major advance, there are sceptics whose lack of knowledge and habitual disbelief can slow progress in getting new methods to those who need them. It has been said that no person will encourage the use of a technique that will reduce their income, and this is another way that progress can be held back. Others are simply not aware of the dramatic advances that have taken place with the successful use of therapies that are not yet part of conventional care and that are based on discoveries that are not yet in science textbooks but soon will be.

The history of medicine has countless instances of reluctance to apply new discoveries. The field of energy medicine provides dramatic examples, as there are still those who doubt that anything can be gained from the study of the human body from an energetic perspective. A different conclusion comes from looking at the rapid growth of scientific literature on the applications of different forms of energy for stimulating the healing process.

As an example, consider the use of pulsing electromagnetic fields (PEMF) for stimulating the healing process in bones and soft tissues. During the past quarter-century, the number of published reports on this topic has gone from a few per year to thousands (Figure 1). This growth illustrates an important point related to BodyTalk and other methods in which the focus is on the use of the hands to stimulate healing. PEMF generally involves applying very low levels of energy, comparable in strength and frequency to the biofields emitted from the hands of therapists.[1] A similar growth curve could be drawn for the therapeutic application of light, with some 25,000 scientific articles published on this topic, most of them in the last few years.[2] Again, this relates to BodyTalk and other methods, since light is another form of energy that is emitted from the hands, especially from the fingernails.[3] These effects have been termed "weak and hyper-weak physico-chemical factors" and are the subject of growing interest in the scientific community.[4]

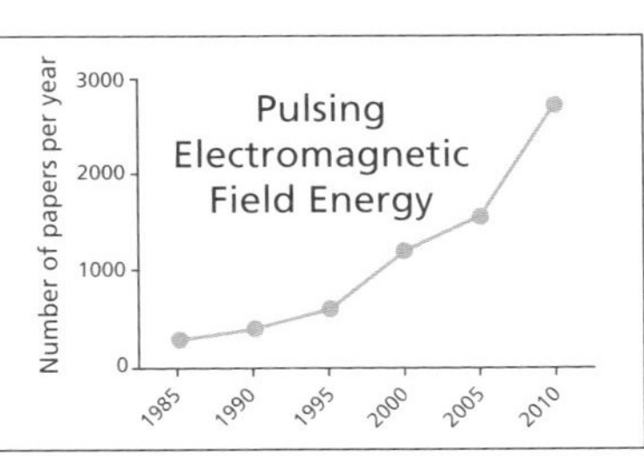

Figure 1
Twenty-five years of growth of peer-reviewed articles on pulsing electromagnetic field therapies.

We live in a time of enormous opportunity, with the emergence of insights and resources that can transform the health and happiness of people everywhere. Fortunately, there are visionaries in the healing community, such as John and Esther Veltheim, who recognize this and know what to do about it. The International BodyTalk Foundation's outreach program is bringing BodyTalk into developing countries around the world (see another book by John Veltheim entitled *BodyTalk Access: A new path to family and community health*).[5] The Access program is spreading BodyTalk techniques that can be used virtually anywhere for both emergencies and in day-to-day life. At the same time, a dramatic change has taken place because of advances in biomedical science related to both the theory and practice of BodyTalk.

Scientists are coming to the CAM community for two purposes. The first is to understand how practitioners are able to accomplish so much within such a broad range of medical issues with what looks like a very small effort. The other is to observe the phenomena taking place to learn more about how the human body actually works in health and disease. Especially important is the way BodyTalk and other CAM approaches treat the causes of disorders rather than the symptoms. This kind of information is invaluable for science in order to determine the truth about the human body as opposed to promoting images of function or disturbed function designed to endorse a particular kind of therapeutic product.

"There is this medicine and that medicine, and this method and that method, and then there is the way the body really is." Kerry Weinstein

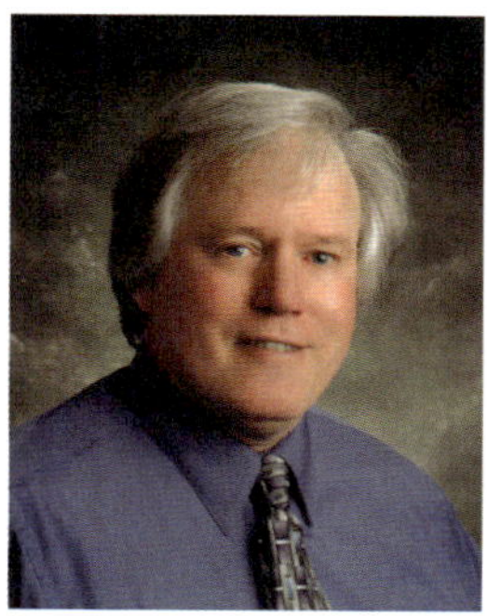

James Oschman Ph.D.
Author of *Energy Medicine: The Scientific Basis* and *Energy Medicine in Therapeutics and Human Performance.*

References

1. Oschman JL. *Energy Medicine: The Scientific Basis.* Edinburgh, UK: Churchill Livingstone/Harcourt Brace, 2000.

2. NLM Catalog: Journals referenced in the NCBI Databases. Pub Med. http://www.ncbi.nlm.nih.gov/nlmcatalog/journals. Accessed November 6th, 2012.

3. Van Wijk R, Kobayashi M, Van Wijk EPA. Spatial Characterization of Human Ultra-weak Photon Emission. *J Photochem Photobiol B.* 2006;83:69-76.

4. Binhi VN, Savin AV. Effects of Weak Magnetic Fields on Biological Systems: Physical Aspects. *Physics-Uspekhi.* 2003;46(3):259-291.

5. Veltheim J. *BodyTalk Access: A New Path to Family and Community Health.* Sarasota, FL: The International BodyTalk Association, 2008.

Introduction

by John Veltheim

My journey in personal growth and what I would call personal awareness started at quite a young age when my father graciously spent several nights a week taking me to martial arts classes. I was lucky to have drawn a teacher who extended my vision beyond martial arts to the power of personal development by teaching me many disciplines such as Zen meditation and the power of the mind.

I was eight years old when that journey began. I soon learned that skills did not come from simply doing a lot of exercises and building big muscles. I was fortunate to have an instructor who realized that the true strengths found in martial arts come from the Energy (Qi) within and the training of the mind in focus and intent. Unusually, I had good discipline at that age to train hard and, in particular, to do extensive Zen meditation practices to discipline my mind.

During those early years, I learned that I could put my hand through a stack of clay roofing tiles without the need of big muscles and hard calluses on my hands. My hands remained soft throughout my decade of martial arts training because I always knew I wanted them in good order for when I later practised healthcare. By the age of 15, using focus and intent and harnessing my Qi, I was able to drive my hand without incurring injury through stacks of up to 30 tiles at a time.

However, brute strength can only do so much. I saw large muscular men with hard, callused hands attempt to break similar stacks of tiles, and only make it through the first 20 because the sheer brute power could only keep the momentum going through those first 20 tiles. By going through the mental process of directing Qi right through to the bottom of the stack of tiles, I not only reached the bottom of the tiles but would shatter them into hundreds of small pieces from the sheer explosive impact of the Qi.

When I was about 11, I taught myself how to hypnotize. It seemed to be just an extension of my meditation practices that enabled me to affect other people. To me, it was a way of exploring the nature of the mind and just how powerfully it influences the body. In this case, I was using trance hypnosis with participants who would lose total consciousness while they were under hypnosis.

Of course I did the normal fun things one would do at school with such a skill! One such occasion comes to mind where, for a period of time I hypnotized a group of kids during lunch hour and programmed them so that in the first period after lunch, when the teacher asked everyone to get out their books, they would jump up on the table instead and bark like dogs! After a few too many trips to the principal's office, I decided to confine my experiments to outside of school hours!

At 13, I was one of the teachers at the martial arts school and I continued to experiment with the power of the mind over the body. One of my favorite techniques was what I called "using my mind to turn parts of my body into steel." I would stand with my arm extended in a relaxed manner and visualize Qi running through my arm out through my fingers towards the horizon. I then visualized that Qi turning into solid steel. Then I would invite two of my strongest students to attempt to bend my arm and they could not, even though others could feel the muscles in my arm to be very relaxed.

My next trick was to visualize the Qi flowing down my legs and through my feet, deep into the ground and branching out like roots. Once again, I turned that Qi into steel so that deep "roots of steel" energically rooted me to the ground. The result was that the combined efforts of two very strong men failed to lift me off the ground or push me over. At a very young age, I learned the power of the mind and just how much the energies in our body can literally control the strength and function of the physical body.

In my later teens, I did several experiments to demonstrate how much the mind could affect the physiology of the body, its health, and its strengths by simply getting the false ego out of the way through the means of hypnotism. However, my goal was to utilize this knowledge and gain a better understanding of how to help the mind and the energy system of the average person, and maintain health and quality of life, in a natural way.

In my early years as a chiropractor I worked at two different levels of chiropractic:

> Symptomatic – based on physical manipulation to mobilize the body and relieve pain.
>
> Traditional – based on the principle of balancing the nervous system through specific spinal adjustments to improve general health. This also involved the concept of allowing the Innate energy of the body to flow freely through the spine to all the body parts.

With the first level, I was basically acting in my capacity to address back problems and relieve back pain. This tended to utilize my osteopathic background to do osteopathic manipulation of the spine designed to mobilize the spinal segments and restore movement where they were previously restricted.

With the second level, however, in my public lectures and in my literature, I talked a great deal about the philosophy of what I would call "traditional" chiropractic. At this stage, in Australia, the public generally saw chiropractors as "bone crunchers" who "fixed" backs. Eventually, over a period of two years of patient education, I developed a practice where less than 20 percent of my patients came to me with back problems. The other 80 percent came for general health concerns and received good results in a specific range of health challenges.

A typical example: One of my patients had been coming to me for about five treatments for general back pain and was responding very well. In fact, I was at the stage of giving him his final treatment when he mentioned that he had been reading my literature. He had read that chiropractic could help stomach ulcers and explained that he had been suffering from severe stomach pain, especially at night, for several years. As the medication he was taking from the doctor was not helping much, he asked if I could try using my system.

I had actually finished the specific treatment for his back pain but asked him to lie back on the treatment table. I proceeded to adjust him using the traditional chiropractic technique, with the very specific intent and focus of balancing the sympathetic and parasympathetic nerve supply to the stomach region and restoring Innate flow to the body. Remember that my previous osteopathic adjustments had an intent and focus of simply mobilizing the spine and relieving back pain.

Two days later, the patient rang me to say he just had the best two nights' sleep of his life. I treated him four more times along the same lines and when I saw him six months later for another problem, he mentioned that his stomach had been normal throughout those previous six months.

Once again this highlighted, to me, the absolute importance of intent and focus in any technique performed on living things. Later, as an acupuncturist, I encountered similar situations all the time. For simple conditions, I often used a symptomatic approach in my acupuncture formulas that afforded me good results in the average case. I had a very busy practice and they were quick and simple to do. However, whenever I encountered a particularly tough case that was not responding after three treatments, I found myself having to shift modes into my traditional acupuncture training. This involved a full diagnostic profile of reading pulses, tongue, etc.

I found that on most occasions, once I shifted my mode of thinking into a fully traditional way and worked out a specific tailor-made formula for that particular patient's condition, I often ended up with a combination of acupuncture points very similar to what I was already using. Again, the big difference was my intent and focus as I inserted the needles. In my years as a senior lecturer in an acupuncture college, I often demonstrated to the students just how much intent and focus determined the outcome of a needle insertion. Simply inserting a needle into an acupuncture point can have a certain predictable effect. However, when the practitioner has a detailed understanding of the whole meridian system and the ebbs and flows of the energy according to the time of day, lunar phases, and gender of the patient, then a skilled traditional acupuncturist can effectively cause many different changes in the energy systems of the body by the use of the same acupuncture point simply by changing the intent and focus while inserting the needle.

Over my many years in practice, I saw this concept to be relevant in almost all forms of healthcare that involve energy at different levels. Another example would be homeopathy, which is, in fact, energy medicine. A traditional homeopath can prescribe a single ingredient that, with his intent and focus as he gives the remedy to the patient, has a far better result than the symptomatic homeopaths using standard formulas designed for specific outcomes. I also saw this effect in applied kinesiology, craniosacral therapy, and the use of machines to generate frequencies for specific outcomes.

My early life experiences clearly demonstrated to me that the state and quality of training of a practitioner, their focus and intent, their clarity of thought, and the rapport that they have with their patients are seriously important factors determining the outcome of any therapeutic situation.

During the early years as I was developing The BodyTalk System™, one other factor, in addition to the above, became apparent to me. That factor is the importance of the attention of the practitioner in any therapeutic situation. In BodyTalk, a differentiation is emphasized between the terms "attention" and "intention".

In many energy-based modalities, one often hears the phrase "it is the intention that matters." From this perspective, intention carries the connotation of agenda. When practitioners proceed with intent, they are proceeding toward a goal with bias and expectations derived from past training and experiences hoping for a specific outcome to the session or treatment.

In BodyTalk, sessions are conducted by the practitioner paying full attention to what is happening in the present moment. The practitioner is there with the client – fully. In this way, attention and awareness take advantage of the interfacing of the left and right brain hemispheres which encourage Innate mental clarity. However, when treatments are given with intent, as is the norm and what I believed in for many years, the practitioner's own agenda, beliefs and expectations inhibit the healthy interfacing of the left and right brain hemispheres.

BodyTalk practitioners work with non-attachment to outcomes. By working with attention to what is required by the client in the immediacy of the session, there is no thought given to the outcome of the session. The BodyTalk practitioner is working from this understanding and has no emotional attachment to what the client experiences after receiving balancing sessions. This is a crucial lesson for BodyTalk practitioners to learn.

I have always fully understood that energy controlled matter and that all the energy of the universe was a series or collection of morphogenic matrices that are all interrelated and interdependent. This means that the only system that made total sense to me was the dynamic systems theory. The term "dynamic systems", in its most generic form, means "systems of elements that change over time." The book *The Turning Point* by Fritjof Capra Ph.D.[1] had a profound influence on my thinking.

It made perfect sense to me that looking at the physical particles of the body, with regard to bringing about effective change of a lasting and holistic nature, is silly. Working just on the physical level was always going to be first aid. This could be great first aid – even life-saving first aid – however, it was still only first aid. This concept will be discussed further in Chapter 11.

It was also just as obvious to me that the body had to be looked at as a whole and that everything within the body, in fact every cell in the body, is seen as having integrated matrices of energy dynamics. On top of this, great care had to be taken to consider the environmental impact of everything going on around the patient as well as the patient's detailed history from all aspects.

In this book, I will be covering how, by taking all these factors into account, quantum shifts that are necessary for significant and lasting holistic healthcare can genuinely be created.

My major problem in the development of a truly integrative holistic healthcare system lay in my own personal addiction to the diagnostic model. All my early training in basic medical sciences, Chinese medical sciences, and naturopathic sciences, had rigidified my thinking that diagnosis had to be part of the healthcare model. However, the diagnostic techniques available simply did not enable a full understanding of the enormous complexity that I faced with the average patient when I was trying to bring about quantum shifts that truly addressed the underlying cause of whatever symptoms/conditions the patient presented with.

One of the key flaws in science is to look for complications in life processes, then add complex diagnostic labels to the complications, when quantum theory, in fact, provides simpler solutions. The classical tendency is to stick with Cartesian models, even in some alternative healthcare modalities. This is fraught with dangers. Complicated healthcare can lead to long-term health complications.

When diagnosis is used as the basis for treating the body, the complex priorities of the bodymind are ignored. When this happens, the focus of the practitioner is on treating symptoms. Symptomatic treatment methods usually end up disclosing further symptoms that the practitioner then addresses in turn, making the symptoms the priority. In other words, the bodymind complex is being treated superficially at best. The trouble is that a symptom has many different underlying causes. When the symptoms are given priority, the causes that underpin them are usually exacerbated and contribute to further, and often worse, health complications down the track.

The BodyTalk practitioner will not attempt a diagnosis. A basic tenet of The BodyTalk System™ is that the actual label of a health condition given in a conventional medical diagnosis does not help in a healthcare system based on dynamic systems theory. Again, this is because classical diagnosis misses so many of the underlying nuances of the client's health challenges.

An added complication when relying on diagnosis is that the practitioner's own personal agendas come into the mix. This can blind the practitioner to deeper, underlying, root-cause problems. Those who work in the field of healthcare, relying on diagnosis as their benchmark, are what I call "classical practitioners." The real beauty of The BodyTalk System™ is that it does not rely on diagnosis.

Because BodyTalk relies on the bodymind's own Innate Wisdom to direct the way health issues are addressed, the BodyTalk practitioner cannot be called a practitioner in the classical sense. Instead, he or she serves as a facilitator, deeply respecting the bodymind's Innate Wisdom, natural processes, and priorities.

Ironically, one of the first subjects I studied in my life was the mind and the power of the intuitive process. I developed a technique I named "MindScape" for my martial arts and, to a certain extent, my healthcare practice so that I could better intuit what was actually going on around me. I understood the power of the intuitive process and further understood that what I was calling "intuition" was, in fact, a specific aspect of the Consciousness that underlies all that exists.

Although I could quite often accurately diagnose what was going on in a patient, I believed this was a skill that I had developed over many years and it was not necessarily something I could train students to be good at in undergraduate programs or weekend workshops. Hence, I saw practical limitations in introducing the concept of intuitive diagnosis into established healthcare training. I fully recognized there had been many medical intuitives tested under stringent conditions to show the accuracy of their diagnosis. To me, this talent was something you were either born with or took many years of meditation and mental practices, such as I did, to develop those skills to the point that they would be accurate and reliable in practice.

Even when I first developed the early techniques of BodyTalk, I still tended to see them as specific techniques that could be utilized by other modalities of healthcare in a very constructive way. Eventually the number of techniques grew and their importance became very apparent through the results that the practitioners I trained were achieving. Through a combination of my own background experience and the very wise counsel of my wife, Esther, who had a highly developed philosophical understanding of, and wrote books on, the nature of Mind and the nature of Consciousness, I decided to make a radical change in my approach to healthcare.

This is when I truly embraced the concept of integrative Consciousness-based healthcare. With Esther's help, I developed a system to train practitioners rapidly in the art of communicating with the Innate Wisdom of the body in order to establish the best way of addressing the needs of the body. This meant bringing together the left-brain sciences associated with the medical model and the right-brain understandings of dynamic systems theory, quantum theory, and Consciousness. The BodyTalk System™ rapidly evolved from that point.

I can tell you without any shadow of doubt, the most exciting aspects of The BodyTalk System™ are its simplicity and safety. The next most exciting thing is the dramatic results that this simplicity can elicit.

This book will take you on a journey of that evolution and its consequences in healthcare and conscious living.

References

1. Capra F. *The Turning Point: Science, Society, and the Rising Culture.* New York, NY: Simon and Schuster, 1982.

"There have been attempts
to establish a Quantum Medicine,
but it was not until Quantum BodyTalk
that the discoveries in Quantum physics
became part of the daily reality
of many healthcare practitioners
and their patients."

– James Oschman, Ph.D.

Quantum Integrative Healthcare

CHAPTER ONE

1

The medicine of the future must be based on sound quantum scientific principles, and sound philosophical and moral principles.

This statement may seem strange at first because most of us think of medicine as being very scientific.

Modern medicine is based on Cartesian principles of science, developed by Rene Descartes, who hypothesized that something can be best understood and addressed if we understand the component parts that make it up. The Cartesian model considers the world and its components to function rather like the mechanisms of a clock. Cartesians believe that if you learn about and fix all the individual parts of a clock, it will then run perfectly.

When doctors apply their knowledge, they take a Cartesian scientific approach and address the individual parts. They often use compartmentalized, scientific research for developing treatments. For a long period of time, this view provided the best understanding of disease and treatment. Although history has shown that this approach could lead to some clinical successes in several fields of healthcare, there are many serious limitations.

The Cartesian medical model ignores the quantum scientific fact that the body is a dynamic ecology of trillions of cells and microbes. This ecology is best understood when using the sciences of dynamic systems theory and quantum theory. These theories incorporate the knowledge that a system (i.e., any collection of elements that can interact with each other, such as the solar system or the body), will change according to the interactions of those elements on an energic and physical level governed by Universal laws. They also emphasize that every part of the system does have an effect on every other part (an in-depth discussion can be found in Appendix A, provided by James Oschman, Ph.D.). Addressing individual parts as separate in function is counter-productive to dynamic functioning and wellbeing.

Despite the fact that use of the Cartesian model for healthcare is fraught with limitations, diehard Cartesians continue to adhere to its principles. Cartesian practitioners are, essentially, materialists who want to specialize in their own little part of the world. Some of them tend to dismiss most of what occurs outside their specialty as unimportant and irrelevant.

The number of surgical procedures that take place in the wake of limited diagnostic preparations is astronomical. However, when the bodymind's own priorities are respectfully attended to, and the root cause is addressed, as is the case with The BodyTalk System™, invasive surgeries can often be averted.

The compartmentalized Cartesian paradigm is what promotes and perpetuates the major crises in healthcare that we are now experiencing worldwide.

Going further afield, it is noted that other academic disciplines also cling to the Cartesian approach, when just a little careful observation reveals that our solar system and Mother Earth comprise a dynamic matrix of interlacing morphogenetic fields. In quantum physics, this matrix is referred to as variations of quantum entanglement. It is critical that we recognize and acknowledge that everything we do has extensive, short- and long-term dynamic ramifications throughout the Universe.

Morphogenetic fields are defined by Sheldrake[1] as the subset of morphic fields which influence, and are influenced by living things. The term morphic fields is more general in its meaning than morphogenetic fields, and includes other kinds of organizing fields in addition to those of morphogenesis; the organizing fields of animal and human behaviour, of social and cultural systems, and of mental activity can all be regarded as morphic fields which contain an inherent memory.

In other aspects of human life, the disrespect for, and unhealthy interaction with, the ecology and our fellow men pits cultures at war with one another and man at war with Nature. Similarly, unethical and competitive practices in trade and economics have led to families, communities, and countries experiencing untold hardships and devastation.

A different approach is needed, which acknowledges quantum concepts such as entanglement.

There is a vast difference between health care based on traditional scientific research and a healthcare system basing its research on the principles of quantum science. The former approach has its limitations. The latter approach produces quantum healthcare.

The BodyTalk System™ is a holistic healthcare system that supports and promotes the wellbeing of any person, animal, or plant. BodyTalk incorporates scientific principles, philosophy, techniques, and formulas to achieve effective quantum healthcare. These techniques and formulas have their roots in both the new physics and philosophy. This marriage of cutting-edge and ancient paradigms has given birth to a revolutionary and highly effective way of addressing disease.

The primary underpinning of the basic BodyTalk system is dynamic systems theory, a forty-year-old scientific model that has been explained wonderfully by the physicist, Fritjof Capra, in his book *The Turning Point.*[2] Essentially, dynamic systems theory highlights the flaws of the Cartesian model of physics.

The quantum scientific principles have been understood as such for more than a hundred years. However, the ethical and philosophical principles, such as those found in the Indian Advaitic Vedantic teachings, which underpin quantum science, have been around for many centuries.

Most branches of healthcare persist in ignoring the new physics and the potential for revolutionary new ways of addressing health problems. With diagnostic models, the superimposition of generic labels and practitioner agendas creates dependency on medication and surgical procedures.

Consequently, patients of such healthcare systems are reliant on treatment that is often detrimental to their general health and wellbeing.

This book is a call to revolutionize health care. There is no reason at all why medical and alternative healthcare practitioners cannot heed this call for transformation and begin implementing models that abide by the laws of quantum physics. All that is required is a shift in perspective on the existing, outmoded, and financially exorbitant healthcare models that are presently in use. This chapter is just such an alert, to all healthcare practitioners and patients, to sit up and pay attention to the gift of new physics that is available to us all right now.

The key treatment principles should be aimed at restoring effective communication, synchronization, and balance in function. These are the basic principles of dynamic systems theory.

All the basic BodyTalk techniques and formulas are designed to restore effective dynamic systems principles based on the knowledge that, if you restore those factors, the body can, and will, heal itself in most cases.

The BodyTalk System™ is much more than another healthcare system. BodyTalk is not just another form of energy medicine. The fundamental paradigm of The BodyTalk System™ is Consciousness-based living. This means living life fully aware of the moment. Becoming more aware constitutes a great deal more than simply improving health. Life is not about controlling the outcomes of what happens in the future. It is being fully aware in what you do each moment. The understanding from living this way comes from our collective mindful recognition that Consciousness guides us into transformation and inner growth.

At present, traditional forms of healthcare often remain out of alignment with, and disrespectful of, the simplicity and wisdom of the priorities of the bodymind. As long as this form of healthcare remains the standard, healthcare will continue to be financially demanding. That The BodyTalk System™ relies on the bodymind's Innate Wisdom, and respects its priorities, is what makes this innovative healthcare modality so effective. It has been shown at Recife Military Hospital in Brazil, where BodyTalk has been incorporated into the treatment model, that patient costs have been significantly reduced.

The chapters of this book will take you on a journey of exploration into how The BodyTalk System™ works from a practical and scientific perspective. Further, they will take you into the extraordinary world of quantum healing where advanced BodyTalk formulas utilize all the exciting developments of quantum theory that apply to the health and well-being of the bodymind. By the time you complete this journey, you will have made a major leap in your understanding of healthcare.

Understanding the Limitations of the Diagnostic Model

CHAPTER TWO

Theoretically, the concept of diagnosis is useful. It involves gathering a patient's case history, their symptoms, lab results, and other diagnostic tests. In this way, the patient's illness is corroborated and named. The practitioner will then use this label to determine the treatment approach. The treatment could involve drugs, surgery, therapy, diet, or, in the alternative therapies, acupuncture needles, herbs, homeopathic remedies, etc.

The flaw in this system is the limitations of the database being drawn upon. In the case of traditional medicine, the database will involve physiological and structural evaluations that are very physically inclined. Even though reference is sometimes made to emotions and environmental stresses, these references are vague at best.

Acupuncturists will also include the meridians in their evaluations while psychologists will include a case history and environmental and emotional stress factors. The big problem lies in the fact that the new physics is omitted from all of these preceding treatment models.

Diagnostic approaches preclude what the new physics has clearly demonstrated: that the bodymind is far more complex than the Cartesian model asserts. For a start, the energy dynamics of the bodymind are entangled with patterns of energy associated with the environment. People who are close to the patient, or anyone who has an influence on the patient's life, will bring about quantum entanglements. These entanglements will definitely influence the health of the person. For example, a celebrity's fan base or strangers who have a powerful impact via the media constitute a huge entanglement.

Family, friends, animals, plants, and electronic devices can also fall into the category of quantum entanglement for a patient. On top of this, the patient will also have stored emotional memories that are still affecting brain function, however well the patient thinks they have dealt with them. Similarly, factored into the concept of entanglements are attitudes and belief systems developed from learned experiences.

In short, when a patient's health problems are narrowed down to a simplistic label, such as a stomach ulcer or breast cancer, a great injustice is being done to the patient. The limitations of the diagnostic database have omitted key elements that are crucial in addressing the patient's ailment in a truly holistic way. A host of unique factors, contributing to and underpinning their symptom, is being ignored.

When health problems are thus diluted and given a generic label, the subsequent treatment model will be equally generic. As long as healthcare modalities persist in using diagnosis as their medium, generic symptoms will remain the benchmark for treatment protocols. What this means is that patients will continue to be treated as if they are generic human beings. In essence, the diagnostic model ignores the uniqueness of each individual and the uniqueness and complexity of their individual health issues and the way these have developed over time.

Healthcare modalities that fail to factor the new physics into their treatment strategies continue to pigeonhole their patients into categories of disease. This is why so many people label themselves "a cancer patient," "a diabetic," etc. Patients are, essentially, being taught to identify themselves as their symptoms. These labels describe only one element of a complex energy dynamic and entanglement happening within their bodymind.

Rigid attitudes and belief systems are quantum entanglements. When a patient adopts the identity of a symptom, they identify with a superficial aspect of their bodymind's overall health. This new identity, "I am a cancer patient" or even "I am a cancer survivor," is highly detrimental. When a patient identifies with a symptom, this attitude can constitute, in and of itself, a health problem.

The categorization of patients as their diseases inhibits patients from coming even close to lasting resolution of their health problems. As long as the bodymind's own Innate Wisdom is left out of the treatment equation, more often than not, symptoms will recur or transmute.

To successfully address the total range of influences complicit in any disease, an understanding of the laws of quantum physics is essential. Healthcare modalities that do not use this database of information and laws are not practising holistic medicine. They are only performing first aid.

To illustrate what is being talked about in this chapter, here is a list of possible influences complicit in a stomach ulcer:

- Harmful bacteria
- Faulty sympathetic nerve supply
- Poor diet
- Overstimulation of the vagus nerve
- Cancer
- Slow poisoning
- Self-induced stresses from rigid belief systems and addictions
- Emotional trauma
- Past emotional traumas still affecting the brain
- Genetic factors
- Environmental factors such as family members, neighbors, community, etc.
- Work stresses
- Financial stresses, and so on.

In reality, the symptoms of a stomach ulcer can be underpinned by a combination of several of these factors. Symptoms are like the tip of an iceberg that constitutes only 10 percent of the whole mass. All the real causative factors of a symptom are analogous to the 90 percent hidden under the water.

The key to lasting results in remedying health problems is to address all the complicit, underlying factors. Currently, when a medication or treatment is designed merely to alleviate symptoms, it is like using a bandage to hide a festering wound.

The problem for the classical practitioner is that it is virtually impossible to establish all the factors influencing a disease. The body and its relationships to the world are far too complex for any doctor to fully comprehend. It is still very evident that the physiology of the body is nowhere near fully understood. There is an even poorer understanding of all the environmental elements, entanglements, and personal history involved in the disease process.

In The BodyTalk System™, it is acknowledged that the only "one" who truly understands what is going on is Consciousness. What I refer to here as Consciousness, is "the intelligence behind all things and the ground substance of all being."

The personalized aspect of Consciousness, in BodyTalk, is referred to as the Innate Wisdom of the body. Another way of explaining Innate Wisdom is that it is the deep knowing of the bodymind of what it needs for optimum health. Clinical experience using The BodyTalk System™ has shown that when this knowledge is accessed, the keys to seeing the bigger picture of a health problem and all its causative factors are generously provided. In this way the facilitation of the appropriate treatment for the client is assured.

The beauty of having "inside" information about the client's health problem is that the practitioner's agendas do not come into play. Instead, this inside information allows the BodyTalk practitioner to address the health problem in a way that is tailor-made, not just for the specific ailment, but also in accordance with the patient's unique circumstances. There are no set formulas or treatments for individual diseases in The BodyTalk System™.

> As stated by Stanislav Grof[3], "A really new and radical theory is never just an addition or increment to the existing knowledge. It changes basic rules, requires drastic revision or reformulation of the fundamental assumptions of prior theory, and involves re-evaluation of the existing facts and observations."

Every session is specific for that particular client at that particular time. This is healing the body in the true sense of holistic medicine. On the other hand, many alternative therapy practitioners like to say they practise holistic medicine when, in fact, they are still making a diagnosis and giving generic treatments that are, by definition, Cartesian in nature.

As you will see in the following chapters, The BodyTalk System™ seems to be the only current system that can truly claim to be holistic because it is based on the pure sciences of dynamic systems theory and quantum theory.

Innate Wisdom and Consciousness

CHAPTER THREE

3

During my years of studying anatomy and physiology, I vividly remember attending a class in embryology. The lecturer described the union of the sperm and the ova and how they then subdivided into a blastosphere of 64 cells. He explained that each of those cells would become the starting point for the formation of some body parts. He then gave a description of the cells forming the brain, the kidneys, the skeleton, and so on. We were receiving an accurate description of what was occurring in embryological development.

Somewhat puzzled, I asked what I thought to be a reasonable question: "How do the cells know what to do, where to go, and why would they do it in the first place?"

My question was not well received! Somewhat agitated, the lecturer replied, "You do not ask how or why in a scientific subject like this! All you need to know are the scientific facts of what occurs. Leave the rest to the philosophers!" I was concerned to note that this limited methodology persisted throughout all of my subjects. Retrospectively, I can now see how this narrow approach served to inspire me to continue inquiring more deeply.

As I sat through each class, it became increasingly clear to me that there had to be more in-depth explanations of the functioning of the bodymind. I was certain that there had to be a way of knowing much more of what happens in physiology, neurophysiology, endocrinology, and all the functional relationships of the bodymind.

Back in the early 1970s, my neurology teacher even assured me that there was no relationship between emotions and disease! Things have not changed much over the years because conventional medicine continues to adhere to the Cartesian model.

This model asserts that all manifestation starts with particles of matter and somehow, miraculously, evolves into sentient beings capable of assigning meaning to life. The concept of trillions of "things" suddenly or progressively organizing into even the most primitive of cells is a major stretch of the biologist's imagination. Any mathematician would be amused by this logic. Eminent mathematician and astrophysicist Dr. Fred Hoyle[4] summed up this misconception beautifully:

"To believe natural processes assembled living cells is like believing a tornado could pass through a junkyard containing the bits and pieces of an airplane, and leave a Boeing 747 in its wake, fully assembled and ready to fly!"

Biophysicists such as Dr. James Oschman[5] and quantum physicists such as Dr. Amit Goswami[6] have clearly demonstrated the existence of many levels of function in the bodymind complex. Their model includes a vital body or energy blueprint that provides the intelligent energic substructure of all the functions of every living organism.

Dr. Goswami[6] describes five main levels of life function:

1. The Bliss Body
2. The Supramental Body
3. The Mental Body
4. The Vital Body
5. The Physical Body

The key understanding underpinning this model is that the creative flow of manifestation is from the top down. The evolving Intelligence of the Universe expresses itself from the highest level to the lowest through manifestations of increasing density, finally resulting in the physical form. In Chapter 9, the Five Bodies and their relationship to The BodyTalk System™ will be presented in detail.

By contrast, in evolutionary theory, the concept of the physical form evolving upward to create the higher levels defies both logic and physics. We do not have to talk about belief systems here or even contemplate whether or not to call the higher levels God or Allah. All we have to do is to follow the simple laws of science without the bias of materialistic scientists who insist on illogical reasoning, in many cases spurred by the fear that something may be more intelligent than they.

The general tendency in biophysics is to use the generic term Consciousness to describe the fundamental force of manifestation.

In the words of the eminent sage Ramesh Balsekar[7]:

"Consciousness is all there is."

Similarly, the brilliant theoretical quantum physicist, Dr. Amit Goswami[8] says:

"Consciousness is the ground substance of all manifestation."

In the BodyTalk model, we accept that Consciousness can be conceived of as all-encompassing. Within the BodyTalk model, Consciousness is defined as the evolving Intelligence of the Universe. The fact that this Intelligence is evolving is evident in archaeological studies and Darwinism. There is also evidence of the accumulation of information in what we call Universal Consciousness. Science has clearly demonstrated that information is not lost over time.

Universal Consciousness is, by definition, the sum total of all knowledge and accumulated intelligence. Universal Consciousness is constantly evolving and all sentient beings are playing a part in this evolution.

For the purpose of working with individual people, The BodyTalk System™ uses the term "Innate Wisdom" to describe the local morphogenic field of the bodymind complex of each living being. This Innate Wisdom contains the information and intelligence necessary for the functioning of our bodies. As such, the Innate Wisdom influences the exploration and growth of our lives.

The Innate Wisdom resides at both the Mental and Supramental levels. At the Mental level the Innate Wisdom is within the subconscious mind. At the Supramental level, Innate Wisdom is referred to as the pure intuitive function which, when utilized correctly, leads to a highly accurate insight into any aspect of manifestation needing to be explored. The Supramental level describes, what in BodyTalk is termed, the Higher Self or Higher Consciousness. A more detailed study of this is given in Chapter 11, entitled "The Healing Nature of Intuition." The Bliss level is the portal between the Individual Consciousness and the Universal Consciousness.

Innate Wisdom is what holds together and designs the vital body and determines the way it functions. In other words, the Innate Wisdom accounts for the "how and why" of our individual lives.

One might say that the Innate Wisdom is the permeating awareness of the bodymind complex. Becoming more aware is a critical function of human evolution. These two statements together seem to contradict one another. After all, if Innate Wisdom is the permeating awareness of the bodymind, then surely, increasing awareness is impossible and unnecessary.

In stating the importance of becoming more aware, what is being called for is a paradigm shift in our relationship with our bodymind complex. While persistence in viewing the bodymind as a collection of unrelated elements is continued, this attitude will be reflected in our disjointed world paradigm.

The next chapter covers how powerfully the Innate Wisdom can be utilized to direct daily life, improve health, and maintain a constant evolution of growth and accumulation of wisdom. Acknowledgment and alignment with this knowledge is what places The BodyTalk System™ on the cutting edge of healthcare and spiritual evolution.

I trust that by now you are beginning to understand that through The BodyTalk System™, quantum healthcare has become a reality. The time has come to look beyond our conditioned paradigm and start using pure science to revolutionize the way we look at healthcare now and in the future.

Innate Wisdom – The Practical Application

CHAPTER FOUR

One important concept that has been seen in clinical results in BodyTalk is that the use of Innate Wisdom has limitations. The key to this is that Innate, as the localized matrix of Consciousness, will only work reliably when the practitioner follows the laws of manifestation. This means that the Cartesian model does not work well under the guidance of Innate. Quantum theory and advanced philosophies, such as Advaita Vedanta, show that manifestation follows the rules of dynamic systems theory and quantum mechanics.

In the basic modules of The BodyTalk System™ there is a focus on repairing the damage done by the Cartesian approach in healthcare. For centuries, as discussed earlier, medical practice has treated the body like a clock with independent functional units. The problem is that the brain learns from this conditioned approach and wires itself to try to behave as a Cartesian machine. The bodymind itself is now perpetuating the folly of not understanding the concept that everything in Nature (including us) is governed by Universal Law, such as dynamic systems theory, and we are not above, or apart from, that Law. Because of this we are seeing the disconnection and malfunction that arises from ignoring Universal Law. We see it in the physical level when we witness organs and body parts not synchronizing well and the breakdown of coordination patterns that are so obviously required for complex systems such as digestion, hormonal balance, and metabolism.

Further to this is the elevation of the egoic mind (false ego) to that of believing it is located in the brain as a result of brain activity. Mind and brain are considered as one. Mind, in fact, represents Consciousness and encompasses the whole body complex. Mind bridges the functions of the Supramental level and the Mental level represented by the brain. The brain is the tool of Consciousness that acts according to instructions from the Mind and keeps the false ego informed of key events in the form of thoughts.

> "Experience can go deeper than thought; consciousness is earlier than thought; it came first. Therefore it cannot be understood by thought." Ventegodt and Merrick[9]

Centuries of training in the perceived idea that the human is superior and "above" the laws of nature and, indeed, can control them, have led us down a perilous pathway affecting our own health and the health of planet Earth herself.

BodyTalk Solutions

The first objective of The BodyTalk System™ is to utilize the laws of nature, as we understand them today, to reconnect and retrain the bodymind complex to the essential laws of dynamic health.

These laws include the concepts of synchronization, communication, balance, and awareness beyond the limitations of the false ego so that the intuitive function of the mind can be empowered.

In advanced BodyTalk, many of the principles of quantum science are utilized in the balancing sessions. These include concepts such as contextualization, re-evaluation, integration, defragmentation, tensegrity (tensile-integrity), and fractal mathematics. Clinical practice has shown that BodyTalk formulas can be initiated in the bodymind that will cause the Mind, through the prefrontal cortex, to utilize these principles in a very dynamic way to restore a healthy mechanism for optimum body function.

Advanced Protocol Chart

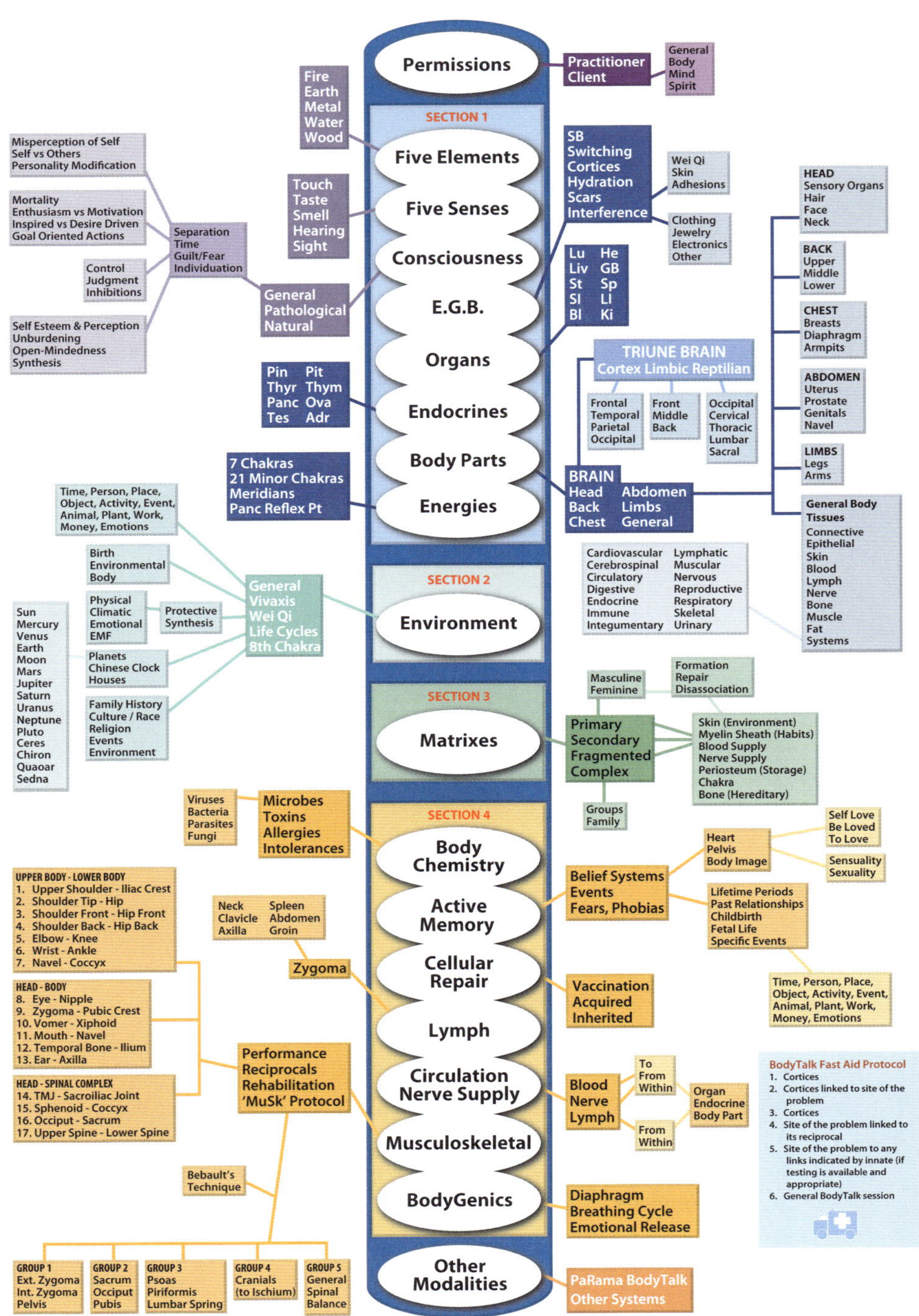

It is well documented that living things such as plants, animals, and humans have energy blueprints that are electromagnetic in nature. These blueprints act like the underlying structural and functional matrix of the body and profoundly influence its form and physiology. Quantum science stipulates: "Energy moves first – matter follows." Hence, systems that incorporate aspects of energy medicine, such as The BodyTalk System™, often focus on changing the blueprint to bring about lasting changes in structure and function.

The main problem faced by a Consciousness-based system such as The BodyTalk System™ is how to proceed. Practitioners cannot simply ask Innate what to do. Although the answer may come through the subtle senses that we call intuition, the answer would not usually be understood until practitioners are well trained in the advanced concepts of BodyTalk. Chapter 11, "The Healing Nature of Intuition" will cover this subject in detail.

To facilitate conducting a BodyTalk session, a dynamic systems theory approach is used. This means a left-brain protocol is established setting out all the key knowledge of the bodymind function, as a blueprint to consult. In The BodyTalk System™ this blueprint is incorporated into a Protocol Chart that acknowledges the accumulated information of all levels of the bodymind from the physical anatomy, the energy bodies, and localized consciousness.

This protocol chart also takes into account environmental influences such as people, work, homes, chemicals, and stressors of any nature. The past histories of conflicts that are still creating detrimental influences on the health complex are also addressed. For example, a common factor would be past emotional or physical trauma that has left energic scarring that is still creating stress and influencing the patient's life.

Procedure Chart

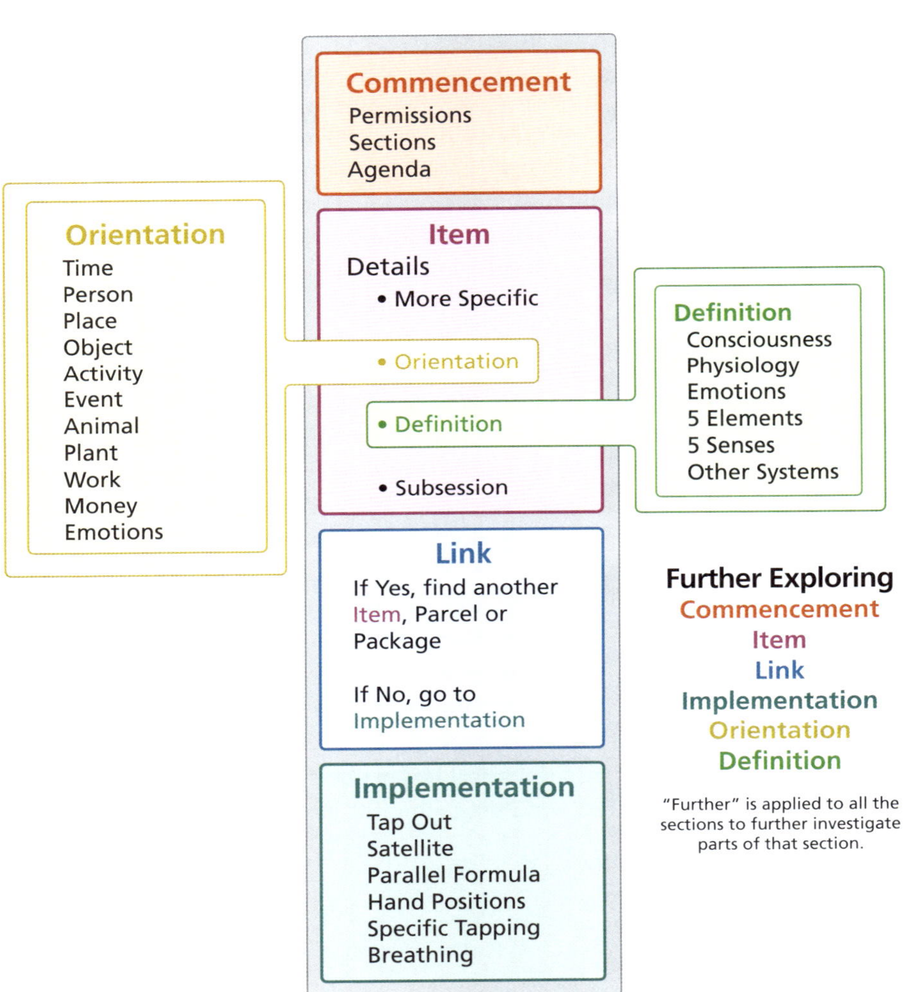

The next step lies in the procedures which can be used to investigate the health conflicts in a systematic way. This has to be in a form that can be utilized by a simple yes/no response from the Innate Wisdom, as that information is easy and reliable to establish. The BodyTalk Procedure Chart follows dynamic systems theory by the acknowledgement and recognition that anything in the bodymind can be functionally related to anything else. This allows BodyTalk practitioners to re-establish connections (links) between any parts of the BodyTalk Protocol Chart. Often these links will appear strange from a Cartesian aspect. However, as the dynamic interactions of the body are better understood, many former mysteries of the operations of the body will be better understood.

The Procedure Chart utilizes basic computer programming principles, such as recursive events, that ensure each section of the chart is fully investigated and that nothing is missed.

For example, a communication link may be indicated between the Gall Bladder and the Kidneys. From a Western Cartesian medical model, these organs have no direct relationship in function. However, energically, the Kidney meridian activates fear and the Gall Bladder meridian activates decision-making. Therefore, an energic malfunction of this link can create a patient who is afraid of making decisions. When the link is made, the appropriate centers in the brain are repaired.

BodyTalk and the Morphogenic Field

By creating the links, there is now a new focus established for the mind to work with. The world manifests according to how it is observed. This is a basic principle of quantum physics. While the body is observed through a Cartesian lens, it will try to defy Nature and manifest according to Cartesian principles. However, once focus and full attention are on the holistic model of dynamic systems theory, the linking that takes place in the building of BodyTalk formulas will establish a temporary morphogenic field (energy matrix) that represents a new probability for the better functioning of the larger morphogenic field called the bodymind.

By the BodyTalk practitioner having full attention, focus, and conscious awareness of what the capable potential is to achieve in a BodyTalk session, that morphogenic formula of probability is now able to collapse, via observation, into the energy blueprint of the patient. To help this process along a focusing tool of Nature called the standing wave or soliton is activated. This acts as a catalyst to initiate and focus the collapsing of the morphogenic field.

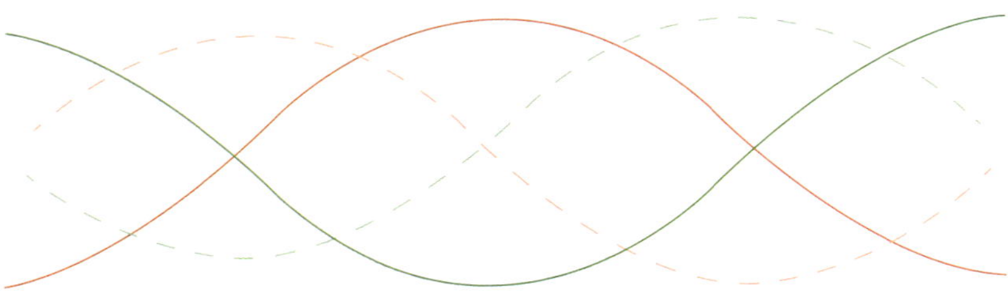

Practitioners create the wave by simply tapping over the head and over the heart complex located on the sternum of the patient. Such a simple concept for such incredible results! Experience has shown me time and again that, in Nature, the simple routes are usually the strongest! Further, tapping directs the energy for the reorganization of the molecules to the changed energy pattern.

Basic BodyTalk Formulas

As described above, the basic BodyTalk formulas are series of links designed to reestablish communication between all the parts and functions of the bodymind. The links were compromised in the first place by many factors such as:

- retraining of the mind in Cartesian principles rather than holistic quantum principles
- stress factors ranging from mental/emotional to physical, chemical, and environmental
- history of previous damage
- hereditary factors
- lack of awareness of the spiritual/Consciousness dimension.

Clinical evidence, over literally thousands of BodyTalk cases, has shown that once better communication between all the factors of the bodymind morphogenic field is established, a great deal of change and healing will then be observed and experienced.

It is essential to realize that, if given the right opportunities, the bodymind has its own powerful healing processes that are superior to any healthcare system imposed upon it. The exceptions to this are in some emergency situations or where the breakdown of the bodymind is too extreme. It is then that the drug and surgical intervention of conventional medical practice has its place in helping the body over the critical patch, while BodyTalk sessions can continue to help restore balance in a more holistic way.

The Essential Principle of BodyTalk Practice

BodyTalk practice rests on the recognition that the practitioner has, in fact, only limited knowledge of how the bodymind really works. It does not matter how advanced they may be in anatomy/physiology, psychology or anything else whatsoever for that matter, their qualifications and experience are still limited. Frustratingly, this also includes me! Therefore, the essential principle of BodyTalk practice demands the use of the Innate Wisdom of the body to guide us through the Protocol and Procedure Charts in developing the formulas specifically for each patient. There are no set formulas for any patient or any disease. Each BodyTalk session is a unique set of links specifically tailored for that patient by their own Innate Wisdom and facilitated by the BodyTalk practitioner through use of the Charts.

Beyond the Basic Protocol and Procedures

Once the basic links are completed to a level where the Innate Wisdom finally has the Mind directing the brain function in a balanced and synchronized way, then The BodyTalk System™ can help further with specific approaches and techniques.

These techniques are still tailor-made for the patient in sequence and frequency as well as in timing of application. However, when they are used in BodyTalk sessions, their effects can be seen and measured clinically and subjectively by the patient in relation to their symptom profile.

The following chapters will explain how a BodyTalk session is done, and a few of the specific BodyTalk techniques. This will facilitate a better understanding of how and why such a seemingly simple system as The BodyTalk System™ can have such a huge impact on the total wellbeing of all living things by simply following the laws of nature as defined by the pure sciences of quantum theory and the wisdom of advanced philosophy.

BodyTalk in Practice

CHAPTER FIVE

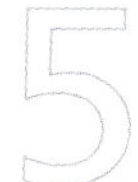

Practitioners are frequently asked questions like "What does a BodyTalk session look like?" and "What could I expect to happen if I were to receive a session?" This chapter addresses these common inquiries. The following is a simple outline of what occurs in a BodyTalk session. The scientific and philosophical details of these concepts and techniques can easily be explained through biophysics and quantum theory.

At the first session, the BodyTalk practitioner will take a case history and ask what issues the client would like addressed. At follow up sessions, the practitioner and client may discuss what changes the client has experienced since the previous session. The client will then either recline on a treatment table or sit in a chair, fully dressed and comfortable.

The practitioner will then calibrate a yes/no biofeedback communication link with the Innate Wisdom of the client to establish an intuitive communication dynamic. Part of the training in BodyTalk is to develop reliability and accuracy in this communication.

Working through the established Protocol of The BodyTalk System™, the practitioner will then "ask" the client's body, through biomuscular feedback, what disturbances have occurred in the vital energy body that have compromised the balance, communication, and synchronicity of the bodymind system.

The Innate Wisdom of the client's body will then direct the practitioner to establish the "links" necessary for correcting the breakdown in the vital energy body. For example, perhaps the pituitary gland has not been communicating and synchronizing correctly with the ovaries, resulting in reproductive problems. The practitioner then lightly touches one point in the link (e.g., on the client's forehead at the energic location of the pituitary gland) while placing the client's hand over the other (e.g., the ovaries) so as to focus the client's awareness on the link that needs to be re-connected.

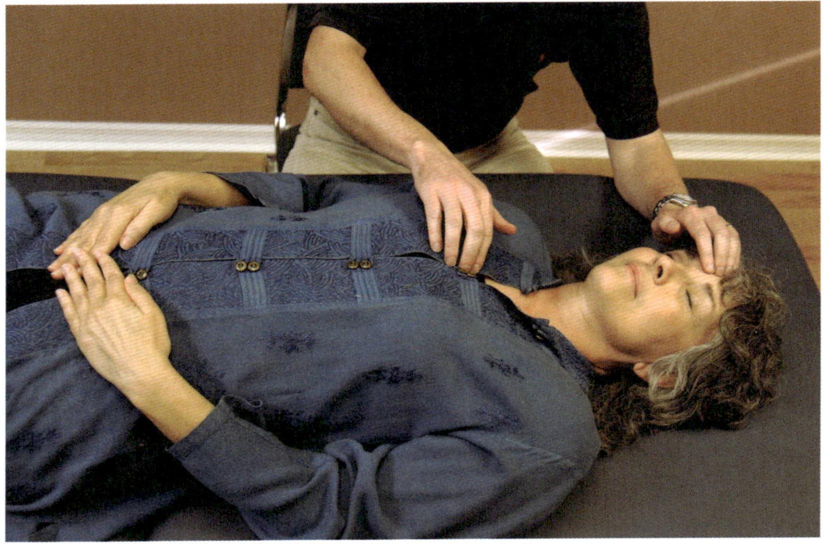

While the two contact points are focused on with awareness and attention, the practitioner will gently tap over the client's head with his fingertips for a few seconds and then tap the heart complex on the sternum for a few seconds. The tapping sets up standing waves that activate the correction process within the bodymind complex. The brain corrects the energic patterns between the pituitary and ovaries and then stores the changes in the heart-brain complex.

Because the electromagnetic energic blueprint has been corrected, the physical molecules will undergo corresponding changes that will correct the condition on the physical level.

The steps are repeated, with the practitioner looking for other necessary links and addressing them, until the Innate Wisdom of the client's body indicates, through biomuscular feedback, that the session is complete.

A session can last from a few minutes to up to an hour depending upon the complexity of the necessary links to be re-established, as a set of links could involve two or more parts to be re-connected (called a formula). The practitioner will explain what is being done so that the client has knowledge of what is happening. Engaging and informing the client in this way allows them to be a part of their own healing process. This helps the client receive a deep understanding of why they were sick in the first place. In addition, the client gains a clearer understanding of the healing process and the role the body plays in healing itself. A client's understanding of all these processes can play a very important role in their return to health.

The power of a simple link, such as the pituitary to ovaries, was demonstrated in a 32-year-old client who, due to her inability to ovulate, was infertile. Seven years of medical care had not helped and she did not want the IVF (In-Vitro Fertilization) procedure. The link, pituitary to ovaries, resulted in renewed ovulation. The client became pregnant two months after the session.

No medication is given and no instruments are needed in a BodyTalk session. The technique is very safe and has no contraindications because any redundant links will simply not have any effect.

Frequently, the formulas involve more than one link to be tapped out at a time. In such cases, the BodyTalk practitioner is trained to focus on the multiple links without needing to touch them. The combination of awareness, focus, attention, observation, and tapping enables communication to be restored between the parts.

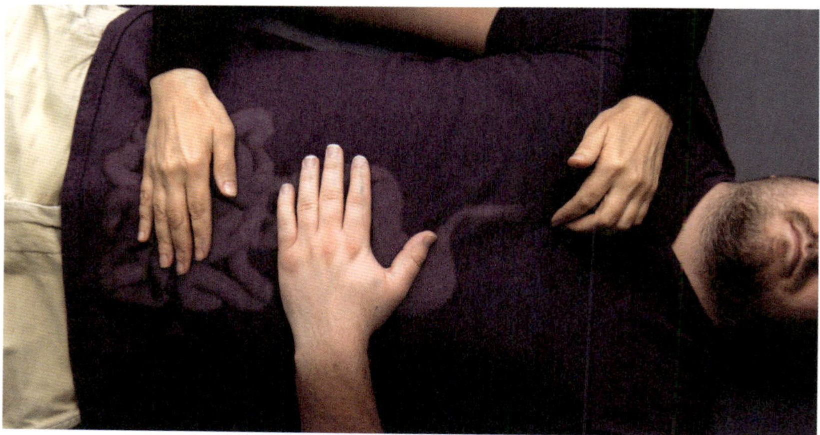

Visualizing a Stomach to Small Intestine Link

The BodyTalk practitioner facilitates the natural processes of the body by allowing the Innate Wisdom of the bodymind to direct how health problems are to be addressed. The bodymind has its own very complex priorities that can seem quite unrelated to the presenting symptoms. For example, the Innate Wisdom might see targeting emotional or environmental issues to have priority over the physical symptom. In this way, the BodyTalk practitioner facilitates resolution of the deeper, underlying causes that have given rise to the surface symptom.

The success of this system is clinically evidenced by thousands of BodyTalk success stories from all over the world. As at 2012, BodyTalk is practised in more than 40 countries and it will soon, in some countries, be recognized as an alternative healthcare profession potentially leading to a Bachelor degree.

Basic BodyTalk Techniques

CHAPTER SIX

Cortices

This is by far the most commonly used technique in BodyTalk. It is the first technique practitioners learn and the one they are likely to use in almost every treatment because it is so important in establishing the general healthy functioning of the brain.

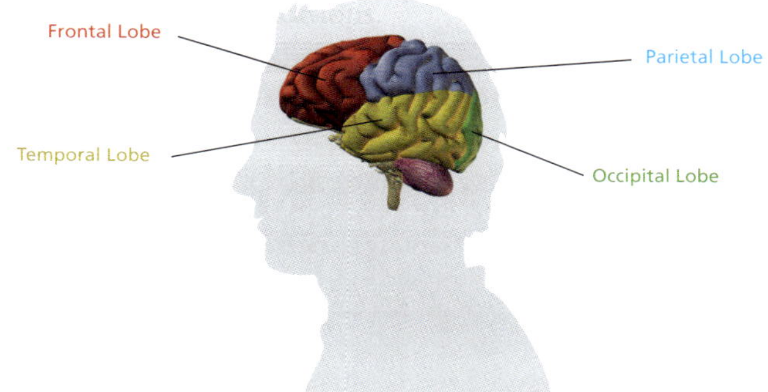

Basically, the Cortices technique involves a sequence of hand positions to cover, in turn, the four main brain cortices – occipital, parietal, pre-frontal and temporal – while tapping alternately on the head and sternum. It can be easily learned online at the website of the International BodyTalk Association or in Appendix B of this book. Its simplicity belies the immense potential of this technique to harmonize and optimize the functioning of the brain.

A main goal of BodyTalk is to have the brain functioning extremely well. When the brain is functioning at that level, it can optimize the health of the body by ensuring the right communications are occurring and the right instructions are going out. However, one of the problems in society is that most people's brains are not working nearly as well as they could be. Essentially, they have been hijacked by the amygdala system, which is the fight-or-flight system designed to keep us alive. Nowadays, the stresses of living often cause the amygdala complex to malfunction.

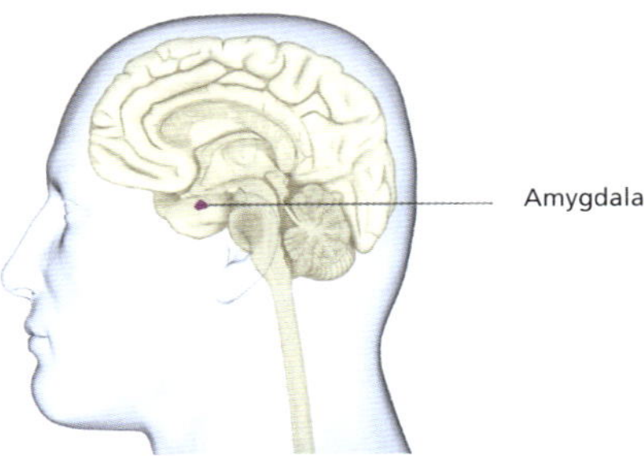

The brain was originally set up to be very good at handling sudden extreme situations, such as being approached by a wild animal. An immediate decision had to be made whether to confront the danger or run from it – hence the fight-or-flight concept. In those cases, you either fought and won or lost, or you ran and escaped from danger and you could relax again.

In the high-stress world people live in today, even though they are not generally confronted by tigers, they are often faced with a constant barrage of hazards that the body interprets as life-threatening. These threats are the ordinary stressors of modern life such as:

- financial situations
- relationships – personal, family, friends, colleagues, pets
- work pressures – deadlines, security, satisfaction, boredom, even the weather for farmers and outdoor workers
- stress of just driving to and from work and trying to stay alive on the roads, commuting
- environmental - pollutants and toxins in the food, etc.

These are all major stress factors that the average person struggles with daily. Besides these general daily stressors, people also face stress arising from their occupations or specific situations. For example, soldiers and their families may suffer stress from the effects of war.

In brain function, the amygdala is responsible for the primary survival drives for food, water, and sex. When the amygdala complex is disturbed, unhealthy changes will occur with these basic instincts. Hence, there is a high correlation between stress and eating disorders and sexual dysfunction.

These stressors affect a person even before they are born. During a pregnancy, the average mother and father can find themselves under a great deal of stress. This profoundly affects the development of the brain in the fetus. Recently, more babies are being born with malfunctioning and over-stressed immune and amygdala systems. This leads to a general weakness of the immune system, increasing its susceptibility to bacterial infections, viruses, and parasites that are difficult to overcome and often remain in a chronic form.

This weakness in the immune system is manifesting increasingly in the development of allergies to just about everything from food to environmental factors, at all different levels and in all different stages. In fact, many people have allergies, yet are not aware of them, because they have no classic allergy symptoms such as a runny nose or sore eyes. They do not realize that they may have a food allergy that is causing their headaches, pain, Irritable Bowel Syndrome, backache, or emotional stress.

Either way, the brain in the average person becomes far too stressed and develops such poor communication with parts of the body that it cannot do its job properly. This is seen more and more in the youth of today who are increasingly exhibiting conditions such as Attention Deficit Disorder, behavioral problems, and major stress disorders. It is alarming how many children are put on Prozac, sedatives, Ritalin, and anti-psychotics when the actual problem is simply that their brains are unable to handle their environment.

Another common factor involved with a compromised amygdala complex is the way we handle stress factors that arise in our lives. Where, in previous generations, most sudden stress factors were handled by the fight-or-flight mechanism, in more modern times the problems tend to be more complex and seemingly unsolvable. Confronting appears hopeless and running away is not a workable option. One example: an unhappy marriage involving poverty and children, where one spouse believes they cannot resolve the marital issues but also cannot leave the marriage "because of the kids." Other examples include any life situation such as a job you cannot stand or teenage children in a rebellious stage. Even a chronically sick child can bring to a family an enormous amount of stress with no obvious solution.

In these cases, the brain often chooses the third option: coping. When we go into coping mode, we shut down and pretend the problem doesn't exist. We internalize our emotions and thoughts and just get on with life in a robotic fashion. This is merely "existing" in life rather than "living" life. In this state, we usually try to experience happiness by escapism through alcohol, drugs, eating, or self-destructive behavior – anything to ease the feeling of helplessness and numbness.

The major issue with this mode is that the internalized emotions and thoughts create internal stress. This is the worst form of stress because it will catalyse major illness over a period of time. Coping is the quickest way to a heart attack, cancer, chronic serious disease, arthritis...and a list too long to state here.

The Cortices technique is designed to bring about systematic corrections to the brain. The theory is that the Cortices technique balances the two halves of the brain – the left and right hemispheres, the masculine and feminine brain, the mechanistic side and the creative side.

For most people today, there is a strong masculine-feminine war going on that is called the "battle of the sexes" by those who misunderstand the dynamics of it. However, this battle is actually going on inside the brain between two value systems or the two ways of dealing with things, such as left-brain logical thinking versus right-brain intuitive thinking. The fact is, in a healthy person, there is well-functioning communication between these extremely important systems so that both ways of thinking can be utilized.

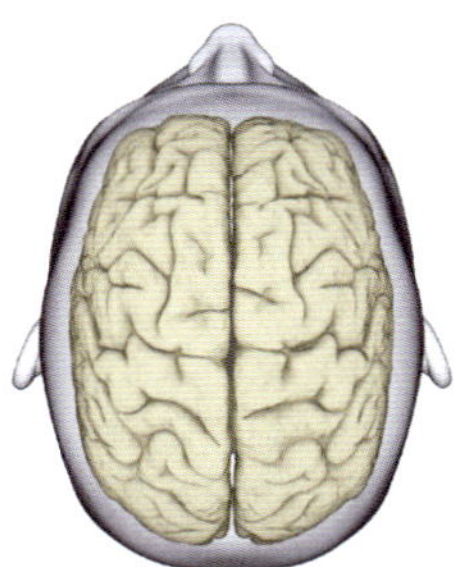

The Cortices technique fosters better communication between the two hemispheres through the corpus callosum, thus enabling this communication to occur at all levels. It also balances the electrical circuits of the brain beyond the nerve pathways.

It is important to understand that the latest research in neuroscience indicates that the actual neurological synaptic transmission of communication between parts of the brain accounts for only some of the communication. A great deal of communication within the brain and from the brain to the rest of the body is conducted at a much higher level through energy systems such as the meridians, the flow of electrons, protons, solitons, and electromagnetic frequencies. James Oschman's[5] *Energy Medicine: The Scientific Basis* is a good resource for further reading on this topic.

The brain and the heart are huge electromagnetic generators and their frequencies are part of the bodymind's communication system. When the energic level of the electromagnetic blueprint is balanced these electrical circuits are also profoundly affected. Further, the balance affects the physical neurological circuits as well. The result of this improved communication enables the brain to settle down and better coordinate its activities.

"The heart generates the largest electromagnetic field in the body."
McCraty[10]

The Cortices technique also improves circulation within the brain – on many levels. Besides the obviously important blood circulation, the circulation of the cerebrospinal fluid and the lymphatic drainage of waste-product electrolytes from brain activity are also increased. In addition, the flow of meridian energy and other subtle energy systems critical for healthy brain function are improved. If this technique is practised regularly, continued improvement in the function of the brain is inevitable.

Another aspect of the Cortices technique came from clinical observations. The Cortices technique has a near miraculous ability to bring people out of the state of shock. For example, it is not uncommon at the scene of a car accident to see people walking around in a daze. From a medical point of view, when the body is in a state of shock, the brain does not look after the internal mechanisms of the body well. Therefore, if such an accident victim is internally hemorrhaging in the lungs or in the bowel, while in the state of shock, the hemorrhaging would not be controlled, which could result in death. If the paramedic at the scene were to apply the Cortices technique, it would bring the accident victim out of the state of shock, and the body would begin to respond and shut down minor internal hemorrhages early enough for repair to occur.

This is why bringing a person out of shock is very important, however, from a medical point of view, this is hard to do. In clinical experience with BodyTalk, paramedics who know the Cortices technique have successfully used it to bring victims rapidly out of shock.

Another form of severe shock manifests as a coma. A person could go into coma from injury to the brain that resulted in physical brain damage. However, many cases of coma occur when the body has gone into severe shock and is unable to come out of it. BodyTalk practitioners have reported many cases in which they tapped out the cortices of patients who had been comatose in hospital for months and the patients came out of their coma. This is just one example of how the Cortices technique could be a vital instrument in hospital settings.

Coma Phenomenon
Marci Hettich - Minot, North Dakota, USA

"I had finished my first BodyTalk class and wanted more proof that BodyTalk works. So I decided to do the technique on the coma patients I see in the ICU at the hospital where I work as an occupational therapist. Over the next seven months, I did Cortices on ten coma patients, and nine of them regained consciousness that same day or the next."

Another benefit of the Cortices technique that BodyTalk practitioners have seen over the years is for people who are in a chronic, mild state of shock. Because of the daily stressors discussed earlier, these people have blankness in the eyes, and although the person is able to respond to questions, the mind is not clear or sharp. These people can function at their basic job and even drive a car but they are in a constant state of semi-shock, which is a sort of coping mechanism the body uses in order to dull the trauma of being in a stressed state. You see an "absence" in the eyes that prompts you to want to say, "Hello, is anyone home?"

With BodyTalk, both types of shock can be addressed simultaneously. The Cortices technique helps repair the functioning of the amygdala system and its relationship to the thalamus, hypothalamus, hippocampus, prefrontal cortex, etc., (which improves the body's ability to deal with stress). It can also bring someone out of shock so that their brain can function far better than before. This enables them to repair their own body more efficiently. When someone is in a state of mild shock, the brain lacks the ability of observation. This is not just about being switched off to the world around them. Remember, to the brain, the body is the world around it.

We find that people will very often live with chronic viruses, infections, parasites, or allergies because the body is in a chronic state of mild shock. Thus, their immune systems are not observant enough to pick up the presence of those microbes in the body and therefore are not attacking them and killing them off. As a result, a person can live with fatigue, pain, headaches, or what is sometimes diagnosed as Chronic Fatigue Syndrome or fibromyalgia because their defence systems are being compromised simply due to the brain being in a chronic state of mild shock.

The Cortices technique often precipitates a major repairing of the body as the body spontaneously starts looking for microbes and killing them off. We also see injuries repair more quickly as the brain starts to function more clearly.

This amazing technique is also invaluable for children who have a poor attention span. Often they are in a state of shock because of stressors from their family situation, school circumstances, social pressures, general environment, and from the additives and toxins in their food or medications, or any combination of these factors.

This is why the Cortices technique is such an important tool in the body's ability to start healing itself. By tapping out the cortices on a daily basis, at least initially, this gradually improves the body's resilience and reduces its tendency to go into shock. The body can eventually be taught not to go into shock except in cases of extreme stress or threat of danger.

This concept is preventative medicine. By utilizing the Cortices technique on a regular basis, the functioning of the brain and eventually the functioning of the body's built-in health maintenance systems will be vastly improved.

Because the Cortices technique is so important and yet very easy to do, everyone is encouraged to learn this technique so it can be part of their daily routine. If you are a healthcare practitioner and implement the Cortices technique before starting a therapy session such as an acupuncture treatment, a massage, chiropractic, or even drug therapy, you will find that balancing the hemispheres of the brain will reduce stress levels of the client. As a result, the patient will respond far better to the therapy and heal more quickly.

Indeed, using the Cortices technique would be a very beneficial standard practice to start any form of therapy. For example, in counseling, where the client might be in a state of shock or stress overload, they may not be able to hear or correctly interpret what the counselor says to them. If the two brain hemispheres of the client are not communicating effectively with each other, the counselor will not be able to make a profound impact because of the client's disjointed thinking and possible misinterpretation of what is being said. As a result, many more sessions may be required to get the same results than if the Cortices technique was utilized at the start of each session.

Oregon Access Experiment
Sandra Wenrich - Portland, Oregon, USA

We ran an eight week experiment in an elementary school in Oregon, in which both students and teachers received Access sessions twice a week. Here are a few of the remarks from the participants:

From a 6th grade boy: "For eight weeks we had BodyTalk. It helped me not to get sick and take away stress. It helps me to be more relaxed, joyful and kind."

From a Teacher: "Students were generally more cooperative with each other (and me) and in better control of themselves; more flexible too."

Yet another use of the Cortices technique is to help with sports or academic performance. Tapping out the cortices prior to an exam or playing a sport will address the stress overload that often comes with challenge, resulting in a far better performance. If children tap out their cortices just before they start a school day, take a test, participate in a sport, or perform in a play, doing so may make a huge difference. This has already been seen in trial studies that have taken place in various schools. In the studies, the entire class tapped out their cortices at the beginning of each day. This vastly improved the level of interaction between the students and the teacher, the behavior of the students, the children's ability to learn, and consequently, the overall grades of the class.

This is such an important technique and it can be done on its own as a daily routine or whenever needed – anywhere, on anyone and at any time. I have included a full explanation of how you can do the Cortices technique for yourself or with another person in Appendix B.

The effectiveness of the Cortices technique has been proven over and over again by BodyTalk practitioners. Yet, it is only one of the basic techniques learned in BodyTalk.

SB Junction

The initials SB stand for Spheno-Basilar. This refers to a part of the skull that is often wrongly referred to as a joint. It is the cartilaginous junction of the sphenoid and basal bones of the skull and it is mobile in healthy people. During a normal breath cycle – in and out – the SB junction moves up and down in synchronicity with the breathing. This very small movement affects the circulation in the brain, the function of the pituitary gland and the breathing cycle.

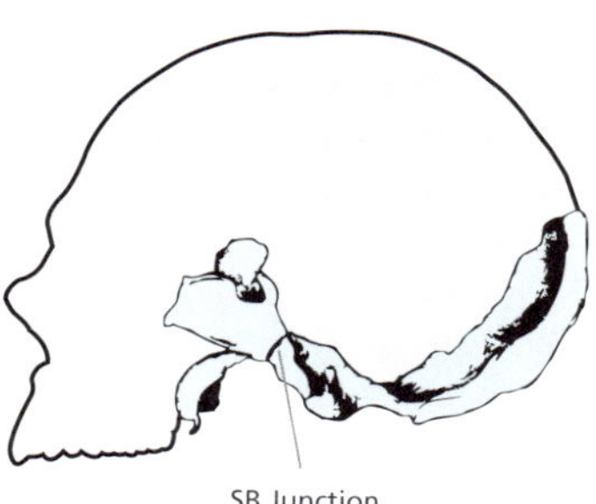

SB Junction

It should be noted that there are two different rhythms to which the skull moves. One is the breathing cycle and the other is the cranial pulse described in craniosacral therapy. The cranial pulse is different from the breathing cycle and is superimposed upon the basic breathing cycle. The brain has very complex patterns of movements that reflect the complexity of its functions.

When the movement of the SB junction is compromised, the brain and general function of the body will be profoundly affected. There are many factors that can restrict the movement of this junction.

One common factor is when a person sustains a blow to the head at just the wrong angle so as to cause the SB to "jam." A typical example is arising from a squatting position and hitting the top of the head sharply against something overhead. If the blow is exactly on the suture near the front of the head that separates the frontal bone and the two parietal bones, then this blow will profoundly compromise the SB movement.

Another cause for SB locking is emotional. If, as a child, you spent a lot of time in a startled reflex, living in fear of punishment, then this will create long-term locking. A typical scenario is four-year-old Peter raiding the cupboard for sweets. Suddenly, his father's booming voice yells, "What are you doing?" Peter has a startled reflex, causing him to inhale suddenly and hold his breath. If this is done repetitively through similar situations and there is definite stored fear of the consequences, the SB will jam in a "locked up" position so Peter will always tend to breathe in but not fully breathe out. The act of breathing out is the act of fully letting go. Peter will learn not to let go in life because he believes he can get into trouble suddenly at any time. He will develop a defensive personality, be hyperactive, unable to relax, and emotionally uptight. This will continue to influence his health and every aspect of his life, even in adulthood.

In an opposite scenario, a football player may be kneed in the head exactly on the suture mentioned earlier. This causes the SB to be "locked down" and the football player never fully recovers. He cannot breathe in fully and breathes out too easily and too much. He develops a depressed attitude to life and loses the "spark" that made him a great athlete. His body will under-function and he will feel he has to drag himself around.

Although these are extreme examples most people fit somewhere in between. Some SBs are actually "locked" both ways and share a little of both sets of symptoms. Minor restrictions of the movement of the SB junction can also occur in stress reactions to life.

The pituitary gland sits right over the SB junction and the movement of the SB is what contributes to the circulation within the pituitary. This circulation is vital for pituitary function. The pituitary is often referred to as the master gland of the endocrine system and problems with the pituitary can have ramifications throughout the body with a multitude of hormonal symptoms.

The BodyTalk practitioner is particularly interested in establishing an unrestricted SB junction because of its effect on breathing. A healthy breathing cycle contributes greatly to the healing of the body. In yoga philosophy there is a saying "Perfect breath, perfect health."

When a person is breathing fully, the diaphragm moves up and down freely with a good range of motion. This movement of the diaphragm is vital to the functioning of the digestive system because it "massages" the digestive organs and helps to stimulate their functioning. In situations where breathing is restricted, the digestive process is compromised and the person will often have a history of poor digestion, energy deficiency, poor liver metabolism, poor sugar handling and many more related disorders. Although there are many other causes of digestive disorders, this one should not be overlooked. (Note: There is also a specific BodyTalk treatment to free the diaphragm).

Once the SB restriction is corrected, the brain will have better circulation, the pituitary and endocrine system will function better and the breathing cycle will improve. This can be demonstrated by using a spirometer to measure the breath volume before and after the correction.

Case Study

At age 35, Vin felt like a fifty-year-old yet there was no particular symptom worrying him that he could actually complain about. He had simply felt slowed down, lethargic, and dull-minded for years. He was a good social tennis player but even his game had lost its edge. It seemed like he had lost his coordination. Perhaps his greatest complaint was feeling foggy-headed, and although his gardening job was not intellectually demanding, he was very aware of losing confidence in his ability to hold his own with his children in computer games and other activities.

Immediately after tapping out the SB junction, Vin said he felt his head clearing. This improvement continued over the next few days. Later in the BodyTalk session, it was established that his problem started in an accident he had eight years earlier. A box had fallen from a high shelf onto the top of his head. He remembered it because the doctor said Vin had a concussion and he could not go to an important baseball game he'd wanted to attend.

Although he recovered from the concussion, it was obvious that his SB junction had been jammed down and all his symptoms developed progressively from that point in time. When he was seen for a follow-up one month later, it was like talking to a different person. There was a glint in the eye and a sense of presence and clarity that had been missing before.

In most cases, it is difficult to say that one particular treatment helps any particular symptom because the BodyTalk practitioner will always be doing a collection of techniques according to the demands of the Innate Wisdom of the patient. Obviously, all the techniques are of equal importance because of the dynamic laws of synchronicity within the body. As in a hologram, each part reflects the whole. Because of the enormous importance a well-functioning SB junction contributes to the whole bodymind complex, when the SB junction is imbalanced, this particular technique is one of the first techniques to come up in a BodyTalk session.

Switching

The Switching and Cortices techniques are closely related because they can address many of the same symptoms of brain imbalance, shock, and malfunction. Despite this relationship, however, switching is quite a distinct phenomenon.

The primary trigger for the switching phenomenon is stress which causes the functioning of the cortices to be compromised. Switching is a natural mechanism that in a healthy person is engaged only when necessary, to stop an overloading of the brain function.

As an example, if you overtax yourself by working on a computer for hours without rest, nutrition, etc., you will arrive at a point at which you will suddenly go into the switched state, signaling that the functioning of the left and right hemispheres and the way they work in harmony with one another is severely compromised. In this switched state, you are in a relative state of shock that is characterized by the brain function "shutting down."

Clear thinking is compromised and there is a lack of clarity. You make mistakes easily and cannot think issues through. What your body is saying to you is that you have overdone it, your glucose levels are too low, and you are extremely fatigued. At this stage, rest is necessary along with food and fluids. Switching prevents you from overtaxing the body and becoming extremely ill.

We can see the same concept in long-distance runners. When marathon runners "hit the wall," they are actually switching. The runners' bodies are saying that they are overtaxed, their blood glucose levels are too low, and their bodies have done too much work. They go into a dazed state in which they feel certain that they can run no further, they lose concentration, etc. What marathon runners are trained to do, however, is go through that wall and come out the other side by tapping into emergency reserves in the body.

I remember attending a lecture with Robert de Castella where he stated that Australian marathon runners at the Australian Institute of Sport have shown that from the time they switch and go through the "wall" onward, they are actually destroying their bodies. As a result, we often see that long-distance runners who "hit the wall" age very quickly. They often have many health problems later on in life because of the damage they have done to their bodies. Interestingly, this is not true for persons with certain unusual metabolisms, for example, some Kenyan and Ethiopian runners, who can run an entire marathon without "hitting the wall" and entering into a switched state.

> "It felt like an elephant had jumped out of a tree onto my shoulders and was making me carry it the rest of the way in." – Dick Beardsley, speaking of hitting "the wall" after completing a marathon in 1997.[11]

Competitive athletics aside, there are many aspects of life in which switching occurs. A classic symptom of a switching situation is when someone asks you to raise your right hand and you put up your left. Or, when driving, you are directed to turn left and you turn right. Those are typical switching symptoms. Others include getting everything back to front or doing the opposite of what you are supposed to be doing. In your mental processes, you are saying "yes" when you mean "no." You make decisions that are the opposite of what they should be because there is confusion about right and wrong.

Switching is in fact the classic self-destruct mode. When you are in a switched state, you cannot think clearly and there is a natural tendency to do the opposite of what is good for you. Thus, a person who is on a diet can reach a certain point of stress and switch, embarking on an eating binge. Or a person who is upset can be stressed to the point of seeking relief through drugs or alcohol.

Switching can be induced by a variety of factors. For example, it has been shown that when a fluorescent light in an office malfunctions and begins to flicker, it will cause anyone sitting under that light to go into a switched mode. This can cost a company a fortune, as employees in a switched mode make mistake after mistake after mistake and their productivity is diminished. This situation continues until the light is repaired or replaced as employees operating in a switched state continue to make incorrect decisions. Further, if something is not done quickly, affected employees also go into the cortices-coping mode of shutting down into a state of mild shock. The same thing can happen in a classroom, profoundly affecting the children in the vicinity of the flickering lights.

Pijnenburn et al[12] state that stress and anxiety are frequent outcomes from working in a setting of intense (especially fluorescent) lighting. Research has shown that annoyance from bright light leads to medical stress.

Interestingly, one of the more tragic incidences we see involves strobe lighting. In nightclubs and dance venues with strobe lighting, healthy, well-balanced people under a bit of stress and already in a state of mild shock can immediately go into switched mode and may start to do the exact opposite of what they would normally do. They may, for instance, go into a self-destruct mode of over-drinking, taking drugs, or just doing stupid things because their normal inhibitions are distorted. This is a very serious situation in which we clearly see this self-destructive behavioral mode occurring.

In whatever way it is induced, switching has a profound impact. Because of their stress levels, many people switch too easily, going in and out of switched mode almost every day, even several times a day, and hence making mistakes and impractical decisions, not thinking clearly and malfunctioning.

Switching in children is very common and obvious to parents and teachers. One of the symptoms of switching is dyslexia. For instance, parents have learned to cope with a child's dyslexia by not forcing him or her to read in excess or do other things that create stress that leads to switching.

When 'dyslexic' children are "unswitched," they may no longer be dyslexic. However, they can quickly revert to the dyslexic state because they tend to switch too easily when under stress such as when they have to read. In such a case, a practitioner would have to do the Switching and the Cortices techniques in combination over a period of time to gradually strengthen the brain and improve its stress threshold making the body far more functional on a day-to-day basis.

The balancing is not designed to "unswitch" anyone permanently. It can "unswitch" someone who is in switched mode at the time of the session, and if done over a period of time on a regular basis, it can heighten the person's threshold for switching. However, we do not want to eliminate the body's ability to switch because it is a natural mechanism that can save a person's life during periods of extreme stress.

The average person under heavy or prolonged stress, however, lives in this chronic state of coping by going into mild shock, coming in and out of switching almost all the time, and thus causing the immune system to be compromised.

I am sure you can readily imagine the value of even just these two techniques – Cortices and Switching. They are of vital importance to enhancing quality of life by helping people to function in a much more lucid way, with far better cognition and ability to think clearly, respond effectively and work and play in a constructive way.

Hydration

Hydration has become quite a catchword these days. Many people walk around with their water bottles, trying to keep their fluids up. This is great to see, unfortunately, however, this is not necessarily solving any problems.

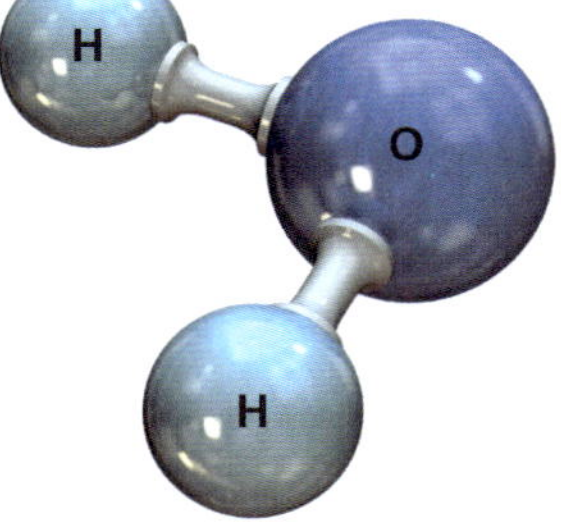

Of the several informative books on the subject of hydration, one I particularly recommend is *Your Body's Many Cries for Water* by Fereydoon Batmanghelidj,[13] M.D. This book emphasizes that our bodies are made up of 70-80 percent water and highlights the fact that water is the one absolutely critical element essential for the effective functioning of the body. In fact, there is not one body function that can take place without water!

- The nervous system requires water for the transportation of electrons and proper communication and functioning.

- The brain consists of 80 percent water.

- Every nerve pathway has a microtubule of water, without which the nervous system would be unable to function as it does.

- Water is the main ingredient for cells to generate energy.

- Water is part and parcel of energy production in the body.

- Water is the main transporter of nutrition, vitamins, etc., through cell membranes. You may have plenty of good nutrition, but without water, your ability to take that nutrition into your cells will be compromised. This means you could eat very well but actually be malnourished.

- The presence and actions of water molecules also control the metabolism of emotions, the functioning of the muscles, and the connective tissue which is critical for the storage of memory.

> Batmanghelidj[2] states that on average, about two-thirds of the human body is made up of water, H2O, with cells consisting of 65-90% water by weight. The percentage of water varies in different types of tissue:
>
> Lean muscle, 75%
> Blood, 83%
> Body fat, 25%
> Bone, 22%

Early in the development of The BodyTalk System™, I discovered that some people can drink a lot of water but still be dehydrated! In fact, they actually show various signs of dehydration – such as low energy, poor metabolism, poor absorption of nutrients, a highly stressed and volatile nervous system, and dry skin – which means that, although the person may be drinking plenty of water, it is not getting to the places where the fluid is needed. Rather, the water is staying between the cells. In fact, such persons could have edema (swelling caused by too much water in the tissues) as a result of the water being taken in but not utilized properly by the body. The mechanism that enables the water to be utilized by the nervous system, or for it to transport nutrients or other elements across the cell membranes, has been compromised.

The BodyTalk technique for Hydration is designed to address that problem: to get the water to be utilized properly by the cells; to increase the transportation of water molecules across the cell membranes; and to be able to hold the water molecules with the correct electrical charge around all the cells, in the connective tissue and along the neurological pathways.

The issue is not about the quantity of water, it is about how our body utilizes the water we drink.

When the Hydration technique is applied, people immediately start responding by showing signs of better nutrition, better functioning of the nervous system, far less stress in the system, and so on. Often, the demand or need for water is diminished and they find they do not have to drink as much and are less thirsty.

The problem of poor hydration has been amplified in modern Western societies where there is a trend for children to drink less pure water. Instead, they drink caffeinated soft drinks that act as diuretics and cause even greater dehydration. Hence, they have poor absorption of nutrients and a tendency to have malfunctions of the nervous system due to the diminished nerve conduction. This contributes to hyperactivity, learning disorders, and weakened immune systems.

Hydration is a critical factor in any health situation. Our bodies simply cannot respond and heal properly unless the water molecules in it are being effectively utilized. This technique in BodyTalk is designed to ensure that effective utilization.

Case Study

Jenny B, a Canadian in her mid-40s, suffered with chronic bronchitis, which was gradually deteriorating into the lung degeneration condition of bronchiectasis. She had constant mucus and fluids in the lung and very severe coughing fits. It was obvious that the cells of her lungs were under-functioning and her Innate Wisdom indicated that her lung cells were, in fact, dehydrated. So although she had too much fluid in the lungs, little of this fluid was getting through the cell membranes into the lung cells to enable them to function properly.

A very important part of her BodyTalk session was, therefore, the Hydration technique, along with several Active Memory techniques for different periods in her life where she experienced a great loss and was unable to fully grieve the situation. After a few treatments her lungs returned to a strong, healthy condition.

Body Chemistry

The Body Chemistry technique is designed to activate the immune system into responding appropriately to factors that are out of balance in the biochemical makeup of the body. This includes toxicity, allergies and food intolerances, and pathological microbes.

Our bodies are full of microbes. Most of them are friendly bacteria doing a necessary job. Others, however, are harmful bacteria, viruses, or microparasites that sometimes announce their presence as an infection. The long term presence of harmful microbes creates a chronic situation that is irritating to the immune system and to the body and can compromise the body's healthy functioning.

Throughout the world today, there are many people who have chronic low-grade bacterial infections, viruses, and parasites present in their bodies that are weakening their immune system and causing a great a deal of systemic malfunctioning and health problems. The Body Chemistry technique is designed to systematically help the body gradually fight all these harmful microbes and eliminate them from their system.

> According to Steenhuysen[14] of the Globe and Mail, "U.S. researchers have identified all 1,116 unique proteins found in human saliva glands, a discovery they said on Tuesday could usher in a wave of convenient, spit-based diagnostic tests that could be done without the need for a single drop of blood."
>
> "As many as 20 percent of the proteins that are found in saliva are also found in blood."

The Body Chemistry technique uses a sample of the patient's saliva. Modern science is finding that the saliva contains the energic blueprint of virtually everything that is happening in the body and particularly the blueprints of all the disease processes that are going on. At this energic level, the body is actually able to measure these detrimental changes and activate the appropriate physiological generation of antibodies and antigens. The production of specialized white cells is then increased that will in turn, eliminate the problem pathogens.

The wonderful thing about this technique is that in any community or family, when anyone becomes sick through some form of invasive process of microbes, the immune system can be activated to effectively fight it off very quickly – much more quickly than it normally would. For instance, if a person with a virus, such as the flu, receives a BodyTalk balancing involving this technique, the illness will often be gone within a day or so as opposed to the usual week or two. I find that very impressive considering the medical profession and pharmaceutical companies are still searching for a remedy for viral invasions!

Another major benefit of the Body Chemistry technique is that it works on food intolerances and food allergies where a person is reacting to a type or class of food. By using the Body Chemistry technique as part of a BodyTalk formula, the body's immune system is activated to overcome this reaction and correct the intolerance.

This technique is also astoundingly effective for environmental allergies. For example, in cases where people overreact to substances such as pollen with symptoms that are more pronounced in degree and duration, the Body Chemistry technique is found to help the immune system to stabilize the reaction process and dramatically reduce or even eradicate the allergy.

By creating a system to treat allergies, food intolerances and parasites, harmful viruses, and bacteria in a very simple and safe way BodyTalk represents a very efficient form of healthcare that will address most cases without the need for drugs and the side effects that accompany them. However, please make note, in cases of severe infection whether it be bacterial infection or very severe parasitical infestation, drugs are sometimes also necessary.

One of the many beauties of The BodyTalk System™ is that practitioners know very quickly if additional healthcare treatment is needed because if BodyTalk is enough, there will be definite improvement within 24 hours. Thus, if the person is actually worse after 24 hours, it is obvious that the immune system is not strong enough to tackle the infection on its own and it is best to use the appropriate drug or other healthcare therapy.

Another very important aspect of Body Chemistry is to deal with the build up of toxins in the system. In this day and age, we have become very aware that a great many chemicals are adversely affecting our lives: exhaust fumes, chemical sprays, dander, mold, mercury from dental fillings, cigarette smoke, lead from paint, etc. The Body Chemistry technique, when used over a period of time, is very effective in getting the body to clear itself of these toxins.

"We've measured hundreds and hundreds of toxic chemicals in the blood of babies that are still in the womb," said Ken Cook, president of the Environmental Working Group, a nonprofit environmental advocacy organization. "Flame retardants, the chemicals in consumer products like personal care products, makeup, shampoos. It's a very long list." CNN Health[15]

There are numerous BodyTalk case studies where people with mercury or lead poisoning or suffering effects from other toxins have had those detrimental toxins eliminated from their systems after using the Body Chemistry protocol over a short period of time.

BodyTalk offers a unique and effective way to clear a wide array of microbial infections, parasitic infestations, toxins, allergies, and food intolerances while strengthening the immune system through one simple and fast technique. Body Chemistry is one of the most powerful and vitally important techniques that BodyTalk makes available to the healthcare systems of the future.

Case Study

Fran P, was a 28-year-old British lady with an identical twin. Interestingly, while Fran was extremely ill with a multitude of allergies, her identical twin sister was perfectly healthy. Fran was allergic to most things in her environment and about 80% of all foods. Her allergies were so extreme that she spent most of her life in her bedroom with a protective bubble lining the walls of the room and with special equipment to keep the air totally pure. Whenever she left the room she had to wear a protective mask to breathe through, and be very careful about contact with anybody else.

The fact that her identical twin sister did not have the same problem indicated to me that it may not be a serious genetic factor. To my amazement very simple links came up in her BodyTalk session. I used only techniques from the basic Fundamentals course in BodyTalk. There were several links to her liver, pancreas, and amygdala. The main technique indicated was the Body Chemistry technique, which I had to do four times in the one session.

When I visited her one week later for a second session she was waiting in the lounge room, without her mask on. Realistically, she was 90% better in all aspects of the allergy. She had two more BodyTalk sessions to complete the treatment. This all happened six years ago and once a year I get a Christmas card from her to assure me that she is living a normal life.

Scars

In this chapter, we are going to look at an extremely important, though commonly overlooked, factor in many health challenges. It is rarely taken into account in healthcare practices. Scars, when not healed correctly, can cause many blockages in energy flow, circulation, and nerve activity that can affect the body locally or have serious ramifications throughout the body.

A healthy scar is one that is fine, soft, not tender and not raised. Unhealthy scars are usually thicker, often tender; often have redness around them and temperature differences from one side to the other. Not all scars that are creating problems are tender or red. That phenomenon is just common in bad cases. However, all unhealthy scars will block the flow of energy along the meridian pathways and inhibit the function of all the areas supplied by that meridian. Unhealthy scars will also upset the energic hologram of the body by interfering with the general balance of energy throughout the body.

Acupuncture has a treatment method for scars that can work very well. Needles are inserted into the scar and in acupuncture points above and below the scar in order to enable improved energy flow through the scar. This can have immediate results and eventually leads to the scar partially dissolving and losing its redness and tenderness. Another good scar technique is found in second degree Reiki that has similar results.

The Scars technique in BodyTalk is the most effective approach because it is so simple, non-invasive, and works rapidly. Once the scar has been addressed, the release of energy, blood flow, and communication to the nerves happens quickly. This, then, provides immediate relief of the symptoms while the scar is healing completely. Eventually, the scar will fade or dissolve into softer tissue and any local coloration or tenderness will disappear.

How well a scar heals after an injury usually depends upon two factors:

1. The general health and vitality of the patient at the time. If, at the time of the accident or operation that caused the scar, the person is run down, sick, or has poor vitality then the scar will often heal poorly.

2. The degree of emotional stress after the accident or operation. This is the most common cause of unhealthy scar tissue. If the accident resulted in emotional stress that was not handled well because of circumstances then the scar will heal badly. For example, the person may have been worried about disfigurement or experienced significant pain that stressed them. In another scenario, the person may be having an operation that is very emotional, for example, having a hysterectomy or body part removed that means a change in lifestyle or attitudes. This resultant emotional stress will interfere with scar healing after the operation.

Another interesting concept here is that very often BodyTalk practitioners find that the connective tissue associated with the scar will tend to hold the repressed emotions locally around the scar. Often, when treating scars, there will be emotional releases and memories related to the time when the scar occurred.

A common scenario involves the woman who had a successful hysterectomy but then experiences other changes in her body during the months and years after the operation. Typically, she will suffer from depletion in the flow of the yin meridians that flow up the inside of the leg, along the front of the trunk, to the head. If the hysterectomy scar blocks the energy flow, the woman will experience deficiency symptoms in the abdomen, chest, and head. There will typically be poor digestion, poor sugar metabolism, tiredness and weakness, shortness of breath, circulatory insufficiency, and poor energy flow to the head causing the facial muscles to start sagging - all because of that scar. But when the woman complains to the doctor that the problems started after the hysterectomy, she will often be told that it is just coincidence because removing the uterus will not cause those symptoms. Hundreds of women have experienced transformations in their health after BodyTalk has addressed their hysterectomy scars.

Case Study

Kay had a facelift and breast implants in a final bid to regain lost youth. The decision to have the operation was very emotional and, on reflection, she realized that it was also an attempt to save a failing marriage. The aftermath of the operations became a nightmare. The breast implants gave her constant pain and the scars on her breasts and face were still clearly visible months later.

In the meantime, internal scars had developed in the breasts, causing pain and discomfort. She could not bear to be touched on the breasts, they felt hard and abnormal, and were sources of misery contributing further problems to the failing marriage. Her face eventually healed and looked satisfactory but she felt constant tension in the facial muscles and she was chronically tired.

The BodyTalk Scars technique was performed on the breast scars and the small scars on the scalp caused by the facelift. Within a week, the breasts were softer and less painful. The facial tension totally relaxed and the facial scars improved. After five more treatments, the breasts were pain-free and soft, and the scarring had faded dramatically. Eventually, the internal adhesions in the breasts also dissolved.

Active Memory Technique

An active memory essentially relates to the concept that past experiences that were emotionally traumatic may not have been fully resolved. Active memory is held in the connective tissue and can continue to influence the functioning of the bodymind complex at a local level (such as in a scar). This in turn, dynamically affects the functioning of any other system in the body or mind.

When a BodyTalk practitioner is putting together a formula for a client, if there is any contributory active memory, it will surface as a priority to be dealt with in the healing process. Most diseases have emotional components – either ongoing or from the past – that are helping to fuel the symptoms of the disease. This is why so many healthcare systems do not achieve the desired results. They fail to take into account the "story behind the disease." For example, many food intolerances clear only after the emotional relationship history with the intolerance is corrected.

Memory can be stored actively or passively in the bodymind. When the memory is passive, we remember and store experiences as simple memory traces. The stronger or more interesting the memories the easier it is to recall them. Passive memory is a healthy normal function of the body and the desirable state.

On the other hand, active memory is a state in which we store the memory with an emotional charge. This occurs when we have not fully synthesized the emotional content of the experience. Our body then stores the emotion in the fascia of the muscles or connective tissue, at a location in concordance with the bioenergetic nature of the body. For example, fear relates to the kidney meridian which, in turn, relates to several muscles and areas of the body. An unsynthesized fearful experience, therefore, will be stored in one of those related areas. In the case of fear, the area could be the psoas muscle or the ligaments around the knee, as these are related to the kidney meridian.

American neuroscientist and pharmacologist, Candace Pert, Ph.D. has shown[16] that pathological emotions cause the hypothalamus to produce specific neuropeptides, for each emotion, that circulate in the body and attach to cell walls causing disruption. This gives a solid physiological explanation for the disruption that long-term active emotions can cause.

For example, in a car accident, two scenarios can occur: the person may synthesize their emotions and fully recover, or in the case of a car accident that was very traumatic, the person never has a chance to fully synthesize the emotional associations because of various factors at the time.

Ten years later the person in the first scenario will recall or talk about their accident as a simple description of an event that was once traumatic in their life but is now only a memory. However, the second scenario unfolds very differently. In this case, the person will be emotionally traumatized by the recall of the accident. When talking about it, they may still experience fear, anxiety, grief, anger, or whatever emotions were involved at the time. In other words, their memory of the accident is still active and associated with stored emotional trauma. When the thought of the accident is initiated, the brain links the thought to the stored emotion. Whenever this happens, the body is stressed, especially in any areas associated with the accident. For example, if the injury had been to the knee, whenever the trauma is reactivated, the knee may undergo pathological change, inducing pain and discomfort in the weeks thereafter.

In more serious scenarios, the active memory is unconscious. In these cases, the client's bodymind is not consciously aware of the memory associations. Whenever they see and/or hear about an accident, or even watch one in a movie, their subconscious mind triggers the emotional association and the person feels anxiety, fear, and other negative emotions that they cannot explain in relation to their current circumstances. Furthermore, many symptoms may suddenly flare up (such as the aforementioned knee), and the person is unable to find reasons for the occurrence at that point in their life.

Throughout their lifetime, people collect a smorgasbord of active memories that collectively compound any health problem they have. These problems will eventually create health issues in a person who seems to have no particular reason for getting sick under the circumstances they are experiencing at the time. The sickness can be mental or physical and may simply be triggered by watching a movie that portrayed an event similar to a painful subconscious memory stored in the bodymind.

Active memory is usually simple to address. It works at the level of the subconscious mind so the client often does not even need to remember the specific emotional traumas. In most cases only one treatment is required to clear an active memory and bring about lasting health changes on the physical and mental/emotional levels.

Case Study

One case involved Mark who had suffered a multitude of food intolerances since his early twenties. He had a list of foods that upset his digestive system and triggered many allergic responses in him. Mark was now 32.

His case was emotionally based and associated with his early childhood. With help from the BodyTalk feedback, he recalled many fights with his parents over food. Often it was because he didn't want to eat certain foods and he was reminded of "the starving children in Africa." He recalled also that most of the fights with his parents had taken place at the dinner table while he was eating. He was a sensitive boy and the collective associations of emotional trauma and food created an active emotional memory in his system.

In his early twenties, he married and started a family. He suddenly found himself in battle with his own child over food. A subconscious link to the stored active emotional memory occurred and he rapidly developed eating disorders and food intolerances. The BodyTalk session resolved the active emotional memory stored in his body and the food intolerances all cleared within two weeks.

The incredible thing about The BodyTalk System™ when addressing active emotional storage is that it does not require psychological therapy, extensive treatment, or intense emotional discomfort. The traumatic memory can be cleared without the practitioner needing to know the details of the event!

In other cases, the memory may be so traumatic that the mind refuses to recall it. Good results in these cases are still obtained, as the technique seems to trigger the subconscious mind into clearing the active emotion without it having to surface as a painful memory. In these situations, several treatments maybe required, compared to the one treatment for specifically recalled events.

The bodymind is an incredibly complex system of mental, emotional, and physical dynamic interactions. At last, techniques such as Active Memory are available to provide effective ways to simplify those interactions and reduce the negative elements quickly and permanently.

We often read articles where psychologists criticize healthcare practitioners who treat emotional disorders when they are not trained in classical psychology. Considering that most diseases have an emotional component and will not respond fully until this emotional component is synthesized, does this mean that no healthcare practitioner should treat disease, only psychologists? Surely psychologists are not suggesting that emotional health and physical disease are not intimately interwoven and must not be addressed concurrently!

BodyTalk is providing a safe approach to handling this important situation. Whenever the emotional condition is serious enough to merit the specialized help of psychologists then the Innate Wisdom of the body will clearly indicate it. In fact, BodyTalk practitioners will readily refer clients who need additional specialized care or resources (treatments, therapies, skills, or expertise) beyond what that specific practitioner is able to offer.

Reciprocals

The Reciprocals represent one of the most far-reaching techniques taught in The BodyTalk System™. In essence, the Reciprocals involve the musculoskeletal functioning of the body.

Among the fascinating work that is evolving nowadays is the discovery that the body works quite differently than physiologists originally thought. The historical tendency has been to think that the skeleton holds the body together, the muscles move the skeleton, and we have discs and joints in the spine for weight bearing. Recent discoveries have shown that the body actually works in the same way as the engineering concept of tensegrity (tensile-integrity).

Tensegrity is a term employed by one of the most famous engineering architects, Buckminster Fuller. He used this principle in the development of his geodesic domes and many other structures. With the use of pulleys and wires and all the right weights, the right self-supporting systems can be created that do not apply excessive pressure in any one particular spot.

Researchers[17] have discovered that the human musculoskeletal system also works as a tensegrity matrix. All the ligaments, muscles, and fascia of the body, as well as the angles in which they are organized (in spiral forms and with various attachments), work in a way that is vastly different than previously thought.

> R. Buckminster Fuller (July 12, 1895 – July 1, 1983) was an American architect, author, designer, futurist, inventor, poet, and visionary. He wrote more than thirty books, coining and popularizing terms such as "Spaceship Earth," "ephemeralization," and "synergetics."

In fact, the body is able to stand upright because of this dynamic tensegrity matrix that balances the muscular patterns of the body to the point that, if the body is very healthy, there is very minimal pressure on areas such as the intervertebral discs of the spine and the menisci of the knees. The spine, as we walk and move, is being held together in a dynamic that does not involve heavy pressure on the discs and therefore would not wear out a disc in a healthy system. In a healthy body, joints should be under tension rather than compression.

Only when the tensegrity of the body is compromised – for instance, because of malfunctioning of the muscles or thickening of the fascia through scar tissue – does the tensegrity complex collapse. Then we start weight bearing and putting pressure on the discs and other joints as we walk. This causes the discs to wear down and wear out, giving rise to a major cause of pain and degenerative problems in the back, hips, knees, and ankles.

My observation in practice is that rather than performing knee reconstruction, re-establishment of the tensegrity balance of the body will automatically take the pressure off the discs involved and create a negative pressure. This effect, in turn, creates a vacuum in the knee, enabling the cartilage to grow back thus eliminating the need for surgery or joint replacement.

> According to Flemons,[18] to salvage a compromised knee joint or repair a compressed spine, tightening or augmenting the collateral fascial tissues that envelop the bones would go a long way to restoring joint integrity.

Empirical findings are that the structure of the body, and how well this tensegrity matrix works, is very much a part of general healthy functioning. In fact, this tensegrity matrix goes into the very depths of the body at a cellular level.[18] Within the cells there is a connective tissue tensegrity matrix that is the major factor in biochemical reactions and physiological functioning of the body.

In BodyTalk, this dynamic is considered important and, in advanced techniques, focus is placed on the tensegrity balance of connective tissue within cells, fascia, and muscles. The movement of the muscles and fascia of the body stimulates the functions of the organs.

The Reciprocals are the beginning of this process of correction. They are the overview where we look at the gross structure of the body and the dynamic balance between its various parts. For example, the relationship between the opposing parts of the body using the navel as the central reference will pair the left shoulder to the right hip. If people have right-hip problems, they also tend to have imbalances and problems in the left shoulder and vice versa. This is also true with the right elbow and left knee and so on.

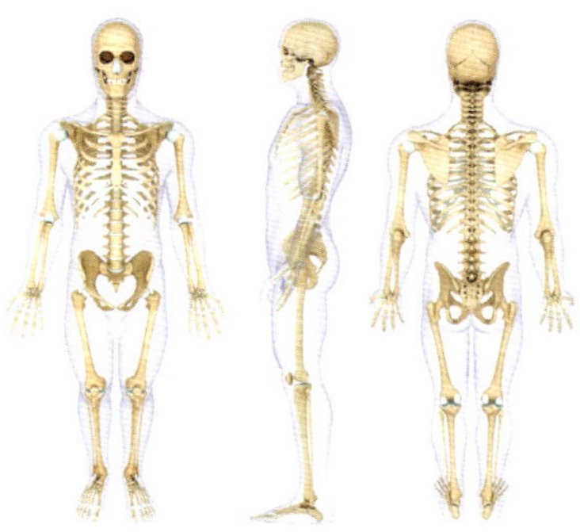

These combinations of points that are usually on opposite sides and opposite ends of the body are what we call reciprocal points. Balancing these points involves touching each pair of points and then activating the connection through alternate tapping on the head and sternum. This simple technique helps to re-establish the tensegrity balance and dynamics of the posture, which will reflect in improved walking and sitting. As the body starts functioning with more efficiency and improved balance, all the connective tissue of the body will operate better: the circulation will be stimulated, the flow of the electrons and protons will improve, as will the flow of nerve impulses, circulation, lymph drainage, and all the different functions of the entire body.

So while balancing of the Reciprocals is quite simple, its first immediate effect is a major change in the health of the body from a mechanical point of view. By first improving the posture of the spine, much of the pain that people experience from poor body posture will be eliminated and spinal repair will follow. More importantly, balancing the Reciprocals improves the general functioning of every aspect of the body right down to the chemical reactions that occur inside its cells. Therefore, utilizing the tensegrity principle through balancing the Reciprocals can have a very profound impact in the re-establishment and maintenance of health.

Case Study

Gary T. was a 35-year-old retired Australian rugby league football player. He had to retire early because of chronic back and leg problems. Sudden movements would cause severe pain in his lower back and neck, combined with shooting pains down the legs. The medical MRI testing showed some deterioration in the spine but not enough to be considered serious or worthy of surgery. There was also some significant wear and tear in the hip joints and knees, which the doctor suggested would eventually need surgery. In the meantime continuing physical therapy was recommended.

During a BodyTalk session with me, two main themes came up. One was to hydrate the intervertebral discs of the spine so that they could thicken up and work better as shock absorbers and give him more mobility. It was also obvious during his examination that his posture had been compromised. When standing, his shoulders were uneven, his whole back was slightly rotated, and his hips were tilted as well, indicating some rotation of the pelvis. All this would mean that he would be creating a very uneven pressure on his hips and knees whenever he was walking or running, leading to progressive deterioration of those joints.

The BodyTalk Reciprocal treatment was done once a week for five weeks, and during that time we saw a complete change in his posture, and significant progressive repair of the joints of the spine, hips and knees. Gary is now able to enjoy playing nonprofessional sports and enjoys good mechanical health in his body.

Beyond The Physical

CHAPTER SEVEN

The preceding techniques have been explained with the emphasis on the physical and emotional considerations, however The BodyTalk System™ does encompass much broader and deeper perspectives within its knowledge base. It is beyond the scope of this book to cover in detail all of the techniques and specific areas of study, however an overview of some other major topics covered in the initial levels will be of interest. It is the inclusion of such diverse considerations within The BodyTalk System™ that provides the practitioner with a skill-set to address the complexities inherent in facilitating change in the bodymind of the client.

BodyTalk is a ground-breaking therapy in that it can also be a spiritual pathway. It is a therapy designed to push the envelope when it comes to "socially acceptable," comfortable standards within holistic medicine. What needs to be understood is that The BodyTalk System™ seeks to address the "whole person." This means that no aspect of the human psyche can be overlooked, be it emotional, mental, physical or spiritual.

Principles of Consciousness

Many imbalances in the bodymind arise from beliefs. The accumulation of beliefs is a natural mental evolution and cannot be avoided. Our belief systems are carried in our subconscious as our personal list of recipes for a successful life. These recipes are taught to us by our family, culture, and life experiences. Each of them involves a list of attitudes, behavior patterns, and ways of living that we think will result in the "perfect" life and can lead to rigid mindsets.

However, just because rigid mindsets are "the norm" does not mean they are natural or healthy. When thinking is narrow you have to struggle against anything and everything that conflict with your viewpoint. Also, the life circumstances of a person may change so that initial beliefs that served to aid in survival and thriving, in effect become limiting and detrimental in the new environment.

Realistically, the cause of your distress is never life, but the rigid, dogmatic beliefs you have about it. Your overall well-being and physical health is dependent on your ability to embrace rather than resist life. Operating with a more flexible outlook allows the understanding that rather than being the victim of life's ups and downs, who you really are has never been limited by anything. This paradigm shift is, in essence, the ultimate purpose of The BodyTalk System™ and PaRama philosophy.

Through the filter of your beliefs you can only see what you expect to see, not what is really there.

Body Psychology

The body can be addressed in many different ways. One effective approach taken in The BodyTalk System™ is to understand the functions of the body according to the discoveries of Traditional Chinese Medicine and Bioenergetic Psychology. These systems developed an understanding of the relationships of physical wellbeing and psychological wellbeing. Many people respond poorly to therapy on individual body parts because the role of the body part and its ties to the acupuncture meridians is poorly understood.

In the following paragraphs, you can read the "personal story" of the knee as one of the main body parts, so that you can better understand that learning about the body from many approaches is important. This understanding, and the effective techniques available to address the issues, are part of the reason that The BodyTalk System™ is so revolutionary in its approach to integrative healthcare.

I Am the Knee

I allow you the flexibility to bend down and move around.
I am controlled primarily by your kidney energies. The kidney energies relate to fear and willpower.

I have always been a strong metaphor for you in your life. I represent your willpower. When, as a child, you wanted to summon your willpower in defiance, you would lock your knees. You learned the metaphor of bending your knees in submission to your God, your leader, or your victor. When you have issues around your willpower, they will be reflected in disturbances in my function.

You use willpower to help overcome fear – the other energy of the kidneys. These two opposing forces within the kidneys represent the two opposing forces of the fire and water balance in the dualistic yang/yin functions of the kidneys. When you experience extreme fear, your knees will go weak. Fortunately, that doesn't happen too often in modern society.

Something else happens, though, that can be more destructive because of its insidious nature. In modern society, the biggest fear is the fear of not coping – with money, work, relationships, health, and so on. When you live continually with this kind of fear, I will be weakened and prone to injury. If the fear is prolonged over a long time and is coupled with weakened willpower to overcome the fear, then the brain will strengthen me by making me inflexible and rigid. You then call this arthritis.

The inner side of me is controlled by the spleen/pancreas meridian. So if you hurt my medial ligaments, it means you are worrying about something you are not able to cope with. (The spleen/pancreas controls worry.) My outer side is controlled by the gall bladder so if you injure that part, that reflects your fear of making a decision about something.

The cruciate ligament deep inside my center relates to the deepest aspect of willpower – the will to survive. When there is injury to that ligament, it means you are often deeply questioning aspects of your very life and existence. This does not mean you are suicidal, just that you are deeply questioning your life, its direction, and your will to follow through and do what needs to be done.

> The bladder meridian controls the back of me. The bladder meridian profoundly influences the central nervous system and activity. When that part of me is injured, it usually relates to your allowing your willpower to become over-controlled by your nervous system. You become rigid, inflexible, and fearful, "standing up" for yourself in too reactive a way.
>
> Your hamstrings are controlled by your large intestine (colon) meridian. The colon controls "letting go" of anything that is no longer of use to you. So if your hamstrings are too tight and get injured, that means that you are fearful of letting go of the "stance" you are taking – to your detriment.
>
> Usually, I start aching in the back when you are going through a period of your life when your beliefs are being challenged and you are afraid to let go of them.

When we treat a joint with BodyTalk, all the aspects of the joint – physical and psychological – are included. By doing this, The BodyTalk System™ is providing a truly holistic approach to the treatment of disease. The BodyTalk System™ takes a dynamic systems approach in regulating all aspects of the synergistic interactions of the various bodymind systems. By establishing better communication within its systems, the bodymind complex is able to correctly ascertain what needs to be done to regain balance and harmony in function. Once again, while the BodyTalk techniques for correcting these important functions are simple in nature, they can be profound in effect.

The study of all this is fascinating. If you truly understand the energic psychological makeup of the body, you then start to appreciate how disease really does develop and why it is maintained. Fortunately, all this does not have to be understood to be able to effectively facilitate the healing of the related conditions with the help of BodyTalk. Through BodyTalk, the brain and the heart are shown what is wrong and the link is established to clear the problem. The brain brings about the changes that are necessary and they are then synthesized in the heart.

Ultimately, the bodymind knows best how to heal itself in a holistic way. Any interference by way of treating symptoms is only a compromise, for the real power of healing lies innately within our system.

General Consciousness

The human being's experience of the concepts of time, separation and fear/guilt is determined by the degree of balance that exists between the aspects attributed to the left and right hemispheres of the brain. While either hemisphere or aspect of mind is given excessive focus, it is to the detriment of its counterpart. This dynamic brings about what is called the "split mind".

To resolve this imbalance, the process of Individuation is introduced. This process requires that the "human being" and the "spiritual being" aspects of the mind start showing themselves to be mutually supportive. This results in a more refined intellect which, in turn, allows the individual to begin differentiating between neediness and practical human needs. Healing of the split mind is all about small, as well as paradigm, shifts in perspective on self, and life in general. This will assist a person towards recognition of their natural state of inner peace and harmony.

Bio-Dynamics

One of the basic concepts is that every part of the body has a frequency associated with it. So in essence, BodyTalk formulas are always balancing or harmonizing frequencies. The Five Element balancing procedures are based on Five Element theory from Traditional Chinese Medicine (TCM). It is a very well developed approach to visualizing and describing energetic balance (or imbalance) and energy movement within the bodymind and nature at large. It is an example of the idea that the microcosm reflects the macrocosm at every level.

Picture of 5 Element or Bio Dynamics Chart

While given the labels of 'Fire, Earth, Metal, Water and Wood', the concept is understood that these are not primarily substances, but rather they are really forces that give rise to producing body tissues and regulating their function: they are the manifesting frequencies of the body.

Using this perspective allows formulas to include conceptual relationships between diverse factors such as organs, muscles, climate, quality of movement (expansion/contraction), life cycle, emotion, sense (touch, taste, etc.) and several others. While the labels initially sound similar to the Western models, it is the umbrella of the TCM paradigm that brings in a different level of understanding.

It is also from this paradigm that the concept of Wei Qi is used. Wei Qi is the term given to the energy that circulates at the surface of the body, where the body meets the environment. The strength and integrity of the Wei Qi determines the ability of a person to interact safely and effectively with their environment. The Wei Qi is further divided into aspects that relate to resisting the force invasion of physical injuries, climatic forces, external emotional factors, and other electromagnetic field energy.

Healthy Wei Qi implies good boundaries. A boundary is a means of effective communication. Insufficient Wei Qi makes us over sensitive to environmental factors and is often a factor in allergies. It is also possible to be overprotective, and to be overly insulated from our environment therefore unable to fully take in life experiences and hence be unable to synthesize those experiences into wisdom.

Also under the Bio-Dynamics heading is the topic of BodyGenics, which is a powerful method to identify emotional holding patterns within specific body parts and facilitating their release. This also incorporates the role of the diaphragm in emotional synthesis and release, with a specific technique for addressing problems there. The breathing cycle, its importance in the fundamental health of the body, and a technique for its correction if necessary, is also included.

The MuSk protocol is used for energically correcting common musculoskeletal issues traditionally addressed with more physical forms of bodywork. It is also used for addressing specific applications of reciprocal theory. Not only does working with reciprocals improve neurological reorganization, it also balances the meridian system.

Macrocosmic BodyMind

There is a theory that at birth we are already "programmed" with many traits of behavior, attitudes, fears, phobias, illnesses and beliefs from our parents, ancestors, religions and previous lives. The BodyTalk System™ addresses this via the concept of the 8th Chakra, located just above the head, which contains the essence of this programming. (Whether this is the case, or whether the programming is only in our genetic code, or both, is debatable. The important thing is that when we use this concept, results occur.) The 8th Chakra is a concept that represents the interplay between the bodymind and the many influences from the past affecting it now.

When the 8th Chakra is identified in a BodyTalk session as a priority, it means that some aspect from the hereditary makeup of the client needs to be addressed to reduce its influence. Examples of these may be:

- family: hereditary illnesses, traits such as chronic alcoholism, emotional and personality extremes

- cultural/racial: cultural behavior patterns (which may cause conflict if a person is raised in, or moves to, a different culture)

- religion: inherited religious dogma, fear of unknown spiritual forces

- events: the classic "past life" experience

- environment: major happenings in a country such as a war or famine will be seen in the attitudes, beliefs and habits of people (and their children) from that country – even if they have been relocated to another country. Disasters such as nuclear fallout, pollution, and or natural disasters such as drought can severely influence the well-being and health of future offspring.

After the tragic events of September 11th 2001, Rachel Yehuda, a psychologist at the Mount Sinai School of Medicine in New York, studied the effects of stress on a group of women who were inside or near the World Trade Center and were pregnant at the time. Produced in conjunction with Jonathan Seckl, an Edinburgh doctor, her results suggest that stress effects can pass down generations. Meanwhile research at Washington State University points to toxic effects – like exposure to fungicides or pesticides – causing biological changes in rats that persist for at least four generations. BBC[19]

These influences often increase the resistance of the bodymind to "letting go" of detrimental patterns, both physical and psychological. Once they are addressed, the results obtained from any treatment sessions will likely be more effective and permanent.

Deep subconscious traits within our bodyminds can be represented by the archetypal energies of the planets. Mankind has related to, and acknowledged, the apparent role of the planets for many centuries. Archetypes profoundly affect the mental and physical health of all individuals. In societies that are more in touch with their history, and more sensitive to energy influences, the effect of the planets will be greater.

One use of the planets in BodyTalk is by linking the planet, and the qualities and influences that come with it, to an organ, endocrine or body part. This will then help to empower or modify the function of the body part according to the archetypal energy represented by the planet. For example, the Sun strengthens and increases energy flow to all that it influences. It also encourages the healthy formation and preservation of the character and personality. So if the client has a physically weak heart that is also having difficulty maintaining the storage of the knowledge of the nature of the character of the client, then linking the Sun to the heart will help improve its function on all levels.

One of the most common observations of the workings of manifestation is the concept of patterns of movement. These are usually cyclic and can work in both the macrocosmic and microcosmic worlds. Some commonly observed cycles include: the yearly cycle of the seasons; the daily cycle of night and day; the ebb and flow of tides; biorhythms and planetary movements.

> "The collective unconscious appears to consist of mythological motifs or primordial images, for which reason the myths of all nations are its real exponents. In fact, the whole of mythology could be taken as a sort of projection of the collective unconscious. We can see this most clearly if we look at the heavenly constellations, whose originally chaotic forms are organized through the projection of images".
> Carl Jung[20]

Consideration is given to the metaphor of the movement of life through the twelve astrological houses. This is symbolized in a few different forms. Some are:

- the 12 two-hour periods of the day forming the Chinese clock, that charts the flow of the energy meridians on a daily cycle
- by representing the movement of archetypal consciousness through the houses, it also demonstrates the daily cycle of energy in the bodymind
- the symbolic flow of life from birth to total self-knowledge
- the movement of relationships through the 12 astrological houses symbolizing their passage through all the aspects of relatedness until their eventual completion or stabilization
- the movement of any new venture (such as a business or job) through the same aspects of relatedness until their eventual completion or stabilization.

Each of the 12 houses symbolizes a collection of consciousnesses, energies, and archetypal forces that give it a collective sphere of influence in the affairs of mankind and the Universe.

Matrix Dynamics

Another framework for working with energic relationships within and connected to the bodymind is the concept of Matrixes. A Matrix is an energy vortex composed of collections of thought complexes, memory associations and states of collective consciousness. In an individual, the most common matrixes are formed by the consciousness (Mind) of the person as a coping mechanism to deal with daily life. Depending on their level of intensity and influence, they are categorized as Primary, Secondary or Fragmented. Matrixes that are helpful to the functioning of the bodymind may need to be either formed or repaired; those that are detrimental need to be disassociated.

Complex matrixes arise between individuals. The whole of manifestation can be thought of as a complex mathematical equation with billions of ongoing interactions and solutions. To facilitate synchronization of all these activities there are many organizational tools utilized.

Whenever several energy complexes, such as human beings, have to interact and relate to each other, manifestation uses energy Matrixes to develop relationships within that dynamic. For example, a football team is a collection of human beings with a common purpose and intention that, in order to be successful, has to develop a unified energy that will enable it to function more efficiently. The energy dynamic evolves into the group (football team) Matrix. The Matrix will comprise the players, coach, managers, owners, auxiliary staff and even the fans. The "football team" Matrix then becomes a useful tool to facilitate the objective of winning games.

If a new player comes into this team, he has to change his style and attitude to fit into the team. This adjustment can be very traumatic if the nature of the player conflicts with the nature of the team Matrix. This is why a great player can move to another team and be unsuccessful on the new team. The period of adjustment can take many games. BodyTalk can play a significant role in helping the player sever from the Matrix of his old team and join the Matrix of the new team. This will then dramatically speed up the transitions.

The Matrix dynamic involves any group of people with common goals or life situations. Family is a major category, with the other Group category including: sporting teams, classrooms, political and social parties, clubs, companies, work groups, countries and cultural groups.

The Matrix technique is most effective with small dynamic groups with definite goals or orientations.

Advanced Concepts

CHAPTER EIGHT

The BodyTalk System™ involves progressive developments in the application of healthcare. The first stage of BodyTalk, which covers all basic modules, is based on dynamic systems theory. This is what has been covered up to this point and involves the protocols, procedures, and techniques designed to re-establish dynamic interaction and communication between all the functional aspects of the bodymind complex.

Because the average person is functioning on a Cartesian model based on indoctrination from the classic Cartesian medical model, their systems can respond very well when BodyTalk is applied to re-establish effective dynamic communication. However, in the more complex cases there needs to be a more sophisticated approach to healthcare. The advanced levels of BodyTalk, therefore, incorporate higher levels of understanding in the operations of the bodymind and its relation to its environment.

The advanced levels incorporate the understanding of quantum physics and the dynamic processes described in quantum theory. The following chapters will discuss some of those basic theories and how they can be applied in healthcare. The next chapter will review the scientific and theoretical foundations behind Innate Wisdom (or intuition).

It explains how the earlier basic methods of utilizing questions directed to Innate Wisdom requiring a yes/no answer can be developed to a much faster interaction. This enables far more sophisticated programs to run to bring about profound changes.

This level of The BodyTalk System™ develops the use of the intuitive process to a level that can be applied in most aspects of life including most professions. It becomes a blueprint that will enable the person who fully understands the principles to be able to utilize their intuition in a very reliable and accurate way in all aspects of life.

This is called Consciousness-based living.

The Five Bodies

CHAPTER NINE

Throughout history, science has put great emphasis on the material aspect of the Physical Body and the world around us. The physical world has tended to dominate science because it is so easy to examine and talk about. Mankind went through a stage of only believing what could be seen, heard, touched, smelled, and tasted. There are many aspects that cannot be measured through those senses, such as thoughts, mental processes, sentience, emotions, and feelings. These are not part of the realm of the physical nor are they generated by the physical. An inanimate physical object cannot generate emotions. It cannot generate the mind and sentience. This simple fact alone should have had science looking elsewhere, looking for the levels of higher energy that are causal to these phenomena.

In Oriental Medicine and quantum physics the understanding is that energy comes first and matter follows. It is a simple way of saying that there is something else of immense significance beyond the obvious material world. There are energy configurations and energy-based intelligence that are responsible for all of the actions that bring together this manifest world as we know it.

The BodyTalk System™ has incorporated the concept of the Five Bodies, introduced by Dr. Amit Goswami[6] and supported by many other leading physicists. The Five Bodies are the Physical Body, the Vital Body, the Mental Body, the Supramental Body, and the Bliss Body. The evolutionary process is a downward flow of Consciousness, through the Bliss, Supramental, Mental, and Vital Bodies, finally manifesting as the Physical Body.

From a quantum mechanics point of view, when this concept is adopted then all of the questions of quantum physics are answered; questions such as why and how waves collapse and how probabilities and possibilities can collapse into physical form. If Consciousness, in other words sentience or intelligence, is eliminated, then manifestation as observed would make no sense. There are too many quantum models of paradox, duality, and non-duality that would simply have no answers. They do not make sense unless the Consciousness factor is brought in. Clinical evidence and application obtained with The BodyTalk System™ demonstrates that this is an effective model because BodyTalk works dramatically as a very powerful healing system.

Below we explore the Five Bodies and review their nature.

The Physical Body

The Physical Body is the final "hardware" where all the activity of the subtle bodies (Vital Body and Mental Body) that are the "software" now has a representation coming into appearance as the Physical Body. The body only appears to be physical because if the composition is actually examined down to its ever smaller and smaller particles, eventually a point is reached where nothing is seen because it is just energy - it is just Consciousness. It is only a representation. It is an appearance, almost an illusion, but seemingly a very real one. If I hit my thumb with a hammer, it is going to hurt even though the hammer, and indeed my thumb, in theory do not exist as solid objects. It is only due to the configuration of the energy, generating the symptoms of pain, and the appearance of a mishap, that the hammer will affect my thumb as though both are solid. If the Physical Body is seen as "all there is," then it will be realized that there are going to be limitations in what can be done.

The Vital Body

The next level to the Physical Body is the Vital Body. This Body covers all of the topics discussed in energy medicine. It is referred to as the "blueprint," "the electromagnetic blueprint," or the so-called "phantom body." We all know of people who have had a leg or arm amputation yet they can still feel the phantom limb. They actually have pain and other sensations from it. In Kirlian photographs of a leaf with a removed section, the removed part can still be seen as a "ghost" image. The phantom body is now quite easily detectable and measurable but the Vital Body is more than that.

The Vital Body includes the meridian system and the chakra system and is a major conduit for the five senses and the subtle senses. Together with the Physical Body, the Vital Body is what responds to emotions. Emotions are energies that can do a lot of good and can have positive outcomes. However, in excess, emotions become something needing to be addressed and balanced. Excess emotions can create changes in the Physical Body as well as in the Vital Body that will be detrimental to overall health.

One of the concepts about the Vital Body, which is primarily electromagnetic and contains all energy fields, is that it also covers the morphogenic fields that Rupert Sheldrake[2] talked about in his work. These morphogenic fields connect the Vital Body to other aspects of the world, to other people, to our past, and even reach out toward our future. They help to maintain the continuity of the flow of life and are part of the whole time-space phenomenon of our so-called reality.

The Vital Body influences the Physical Body in many ways. One of the simplest illustrations is the school experiment done to demonstrate how magnetism works by placing a bar magnet on a sheet of paper and sprinkling iron filings over it. Tapping on the paper will cause the iron filings to arrange themselves in the shape of the magnetic field of the magnet, revealing the curves of that field. If the magnet is then moved and the paper is tapped again the iron filings will reorganize themselves into the same shape in the new location. By introducing more magnets, fancier patterns will emerge as the magnetic fields crisscross each other.

This is an example of how an invisible magnetic field can move iron filings that are visible and solid objects with billions of atoms in them. If we try to examine the human energy blueprint with our physical eyes, we are not able to see it, just as we cannot see the magnetic field that holds the iron filings. Changing the blueprint by using energy techniques such as BodyTalk, acupuncture, or homeopathy, can actually cause a change in the human energy field in a significant way. The cells and molecules shift just like the iron filings, and changes occur in the physical structure of the cells.

One thing that is understood about body chemistry and physiology is that most biomechanical reactions are very mechanical in nature, such as when two substances come together to form an enzyme or hormone. It is literally two shapes that have to "clip" together in order for something to occur. If the shapes are changed, then the body chemistry is changed. This changes what is produced and how much is produced. By changing the energy patterns, the structure is changed and, therefore, the function is changed, which determines the biochemistry and the physiology of the body. So, the Physical Body is profoundly influenced by changes being made at the Vital Body level. The Vital Body works to effect changes in other ways, too. However, the changing of energy patterns is just one example of the many ways in which science can explain the enormous effectiveness of energy medicine techniques, such as BodyTalk, homeopathy, acupuncture, and kinesiology.

The Mental Body

The Mental Body is about Mind and meaning. It gives meaning to the Vital Body and the Physical Body. The Mind is separate from the brain. Neurophysiology studies have been unable to establish where the Mind resides or even where thoughts originate. It is the Mind or the Mental Body that influences the physical brain and drives response. It is constantly giving meaning to what we do and how we do it. The brain then becomes the medium through which this meaning is represented. Once the meaning is received, the brain then acts upon it, sending an impulse to the nervous system to produce a response to that meaning given by the Mental Body.

Emotions begin in the Mental Body. According to the work by Candace Pert[16] Ph.D., when emotions are strong, the hypothalamus in the brain starts to produce neuropeptides that represent each of the emotions. This results in physical representations of the basic emotions of joy, sadness, anger, fear, worry, and grief. These neuropeptides travel through the bloodstream and the lymphatic stream, attaching themselves to cells in different parts of the body and begin to influence their function. This is a straight physiological explanation for how emotions can profoundly affect us. If there is a flood of "anger" neuropeptides attaching to a cell wall, the absorption of all of the other nutrients into the cell will be restricted, causing that cell to malfunction.

When we speak of "hearing" thoughts in our heads, we are referring to the subtle sense of sound, as those thoughts are not received through our ears. The physical brain does not produce thoughts. Thoughts appear to come from the "Supramental" Consciousness which will be discussed later. Essentially, the brain is like a receiver of thoughts similar to a radio station receiving a broadcast. The thoughts are coming from the aspect of Universal Consciousness that is related to us.

Bruce Lipton,[21] Ph.D., refers to small outcroppings on cell walls that function as antennae. These receive information in the form of electromagnetic frequencies, like radio antennae. Every cell has this structure so that cells are able to communicate with each other. The brain cells, in particular, are able to communicate by receiving information from what is referred to as our "Higher Self" or the Supramental Body.

The key element at the mental level is that, at this stage, life appears messy and unpredictable. The Mental Body is unable to ascribe enough meaning or think within a broad enough contextual framework to understand what is really going on in life and in our physical reality. Bridging the gap requires a certain amount of intuitive processing, which is a way of communicating with our Higher Self and other people's Higher Selves. This communication can become quite accurate by using certain techniques. However, at the Mental Body level, that intuition is not going to be as reliable because the big picture is not understood.

The Supramental Body

This is the highest level that can be easily accessed with training. This level is also known as the Higher Self and Supramental Intellect. It is a domain of much greater awareness compared to the mental level. We talk about gradually learning through life and acquiring wisdom, developing a deeper understanding of life, and seeing the big picture. Through that understanding and perception, we start to become more in touch with our Higher Self, more in touch with our wisdom and our intuition. Some people will be much more in touch with it than others. Others will rarely access it because they are so focused on the material world and they use the Mental Body as their highest resource.

Via the laws of quantum physics, the phenomena of the Supramental Body level are just beginning to be understood. It is the level at which manifestation into physicality occurs. In fact, one of the key manifestations of the Supramental Body is to provide contextual frameworks for mental meanings and vital functions. It is not enough to just have meaning and function. Things need to be able to be put into context. Often, mistakes are made simply because the big picture is unable to be seen. For example, what may be appropriate behavior in one situation could be inappropriate in another. This is the difference between being at a party and yelling out and being in a library and yelling out.

On deeper levels, the brain and body systems may begin to function in the wrong context, causing overreactions to situations that, in turn, create allergies and stresses. Very often those stresses are purely because of a lack of understanding of the context of what is going on and an inability to evaluate it properly. The concept of the Supramental Body is that of a processor that is constantly evaluating and re-evaluating what is going on, trying to put things into context. When this aspect is operating efficiently, the Mental Body functions far better which then influences the Vital Body through to the Physical Body. Our whole wellbeing will be greatly improved.

The Supramental Body level, therefore, is the center of the advanced intuition. Here, the intuitive processes are so real and so firm. This is also referred to as insight. This is when "we know without any shadow of doubt" or when "we would stake our life on it." It is that type of intuition. Very few people experience that more than once or twice in a lifetime because most people tend to work at the Mental Body level. When working at the Supramental level, that kind of intuition can happen frequently and is what helps achieve success in life across all avenues. The reality is that Supramental intuition is far more reliable than any left-brain form of analysis or understanding.

The Supramental Body sees the synchronicity of life and understands it. When operating from the Supramental level all of the little events in life and why they happen are revealed. Understanding begins to emerge regarding how the occurrence of one event leads to the next and the realization that life is not a whole bunch of coincidences. There are, in fact, very few coincidences. When something is lost or an illness or injury sustained, one of the key elements in the healing process is to be able to understand why that happened – what was behind it? What process was occurring? What were the sources that caused the development of that illness?

The paradigm of The BodyTalk System™ maintains that when the true etiology of disease is fully understood, and all the causative factors re-evaluated and put into context, the body is then capable of healing itself. The body will be able to heal itself even from the most serious illnesses – practitioners just need to know the techniques for clarification.

One of the interesting aspects of the Supramental intellect is the concept of feelings. It is at the Supramental level that feelings are synthesized. These feelings are called inner processing. The reality is that most people do not understand the difference between emotions and feelings.

Examples of emotions are anger, fear, worry, sadness, or grief. These are the strong emotions. Sometimes they are called different names such as depression, rejection, shame, envy, and frustration. These emotions are quite distinct. One can say, "I am angry" or "I am grieving because my dog just died." Emotions are there for a purpose and when they function normally they are best left alone. If emotions are functioning abnormally, the person is overreacting and that affects their health. This is when interventions are used. Doctors will attempt to administer medications, a psychologist will use counseling, and a BodyTalk practitioner will use concepts like the BreakThrough program and other BodyTalk techniques to help speed up the process in synthesizing whatever is out of balance.

Feelings are a different concept. They occur at a higher level, the Supramental level. As a result they are not really emotions, but rather an inner processing. They may appear to be like emotions because as major shifts are processed, in essence letting go of an aspect of our life, there is a very subtle form of grieving occurring. It is grieving over the shift from one way of limited thinking to an alternative level of awareness.

During a therapy session, whether in psychotherapy, a BodyTalk session, or other modalities, a point may be reached when a paradigm shift occurs. Feelings arise that bring about an internal process of resolution where the patient will become very quiet. There will probably be a couple of tears in their eyes and they are choked up. They are in this processing stage.

As key to this situation, feelings should never be treated. Feelings, when they operate properly, are in fact the treatment. They enable movement from one way of living into another way of being; from one set of belief systems, attitudes, and concepts to a completely different set because things have been put in a different context. A re-evaluation of a person's life has occurred, in however large or small a way.

I am always horrified when I hear about so many therapists dealing with a client who is going into the feeling mode and they ask the big question, "What are you feeling? Describe your feeling." This approach is usually unproductive. Asking a client about their feelings is inappropriate because they simply cannot express them. They do not know what they are feeling. If a practitioner or therapist persists in asking, the client is going to make something up that will have emotional implications. More importantly, what they usually do is shut down their feelings and shut down that process.

What could have been a very good counseling session or BodyTalk session may literally have been destroyed because the practitioner has not allowed synthesis of the therapeutic intervention; the "a ha" paradigm shift to come to fruition so that the client can heal themselves.

> The heart and brain maintain a continuous two-way dialogue, each influencing the other's functioning. The signals the heart sends to the brain can influence perception, emotional processing, and higher cognitive functions. This system and circuitry is viewed by neurocardiology researchers as a "heart brain." Institute of HeartMath[22]

That question pulls the client out of the process and denies them the real benefit of the therapeutic intervention. The Supramental intellect appears to reside in the heart energy complex. It has been established[22] that the heart can also be referred to as the heart-brain as evidence is clear that the heart contains many neurons of a highly complex structure. In Chinese medicine, the energy in the heart is called the Shen, and is considered the seat of awareness of the body – particularly the seat of self-awareness. This concept has been further elaborated in bioenergetic psychology, BodyTalk, Advaita Vedanta philosophy, and biophysics, the premise being that significant changes that occur in the bodymind complex are reflected in the heart-brain. The heart-brain complex then maintains those changes and constantly communicates the essence of those changes to all the cells in the body. This communication appears to be encoded in the frequencies of the pulse of the heart, as evidenced in Chinese pulse diagnosis, through the meridian system, bio-electromagnetic frequency transmission, and by resonance.

During my own journey in developing BodyTalk, I was faced with the age-old problem of healthcare, which is the need to maintain the effectiveness of a treatment. Often treatments had to be repeated several times before they had lasting effect. Once I utilized the concept of tapping over the heart complex with the intent and focus of embedding the essential wisdom of the treatment into the heart complex, there was no longer a need to repeat formulas.

Given this premise, it appears that the heart complex plays a major role in the interaction of Mind and brain. The work of Richard Amoroso[23] and his colleagues would indicate that the Mind incorporates the total functioning of the heart-brain together with the brain located in the head. As such, it uses this "bigger picture" to establish what instructions to give the brain for day-to-day functioning. Dr. Amoroso[23] has established that the Mind interfaces with the brain in quantum microtubule events.

I propose that the Supramental intellect be defined as a combination of the total Mind mentioned above, combined with its link to Universal Consciousness and its relative awareness of all the other Supramental intellects surrounding it. As such, it has the resources for making the decisions and corrections for any life processes.

The "false ego" is defined as our awareness of being a "somebody". When we say "me" or "I" and all that comes with that concept, we are referring to the false ego, which is part of brain function. According to the research of Francis Crick and Christof Koch,[24] it is located in a thin membrane at the base of the cortices called the claustrum.

The false ego is constantly receiving information of all activity in the brain and assuming responsibility for it. As such, it believes that it is the creator of the thoughts, ideas, and decisions that are being made. Whereas, in reality, it would appear that it is simply monitoring events and giving us a false sense of being the actual doer, hence why many philosophies talk about the concept that we are only the observer of all activity and have no actual control over anything that occurs because everything we observe is retrospective by the time we have observed it.

In the big picture, the Supramental intellect is where the "action" occurs. This is where decisions are made because only at this level can there be an awareness of all the factors required for any appropriate action. The Supramental level recognizes that all actions are synchronized with everything that is going on in manifestation. This implies that all decisions will not necessarily be of primary advantage to each individual because, ultimately, life processes are always about the big picture.

These concepts can be quite confrontational and are addressed just briefly here. The BodyTalk System™ teaches this subject in far more detail in our advanced courses. The deeper the practitioners' understanding of the functioning of manifestation, the more useful they will be as facilitators for appropriate changes in patients.

The Bliss Body

Bliss is a term that is often used in philosophy and science. It could be called the highest level of Consciousness that is still related to a particular Body. It is the foundation of all of the unlimited possibilities and potentials at the moment of birth. In fetal life, before the physical development has completely manifested, the Bliss Body contains a tremendous variety of potential for existence. There is a tremendous amount of quantum probabilities and possibilities. As the fetus develops, each of the other four Bodies (Supramental Body, Mental Body, Vital Body, and Physical Body), in turn, increasingly narrow down and create limitations on these possibilities. The final Physical Body is the most limited version of the whole person. The entire body is made up of these five levels - not just the one physical level.

At the Bliss level, there is oneness with the order of life. It is a feedback center for the lower bodies. It is a feedback mechanism that encompasses the deep wisdom of Universal Consciousness. At that level, the healing that takes place is called "spiritual" healing. It is more like the spontaneous remissions or miracles that are seen occasionally or heard about in history studies and discussed in certain religions.

Healing the Five Bodies

CHAPTER TEN

10

At this stage, this whole set-up of the Five Bodies needs to be examined and understood, focusing around what the relationships among them means when it comes to the various healthcare modalities throughout the world. Remember that all creative processes, and therefore healing processes, must originate from the highest body and flow down to the lower ones because the laws of physics dictate so. They cannot be spawned by the Physical Body and flow up the ladder of Consciousness; that is like saying a table knows how to heal somebody. Consciousness flows down, not up.

There are systems of therapy that work at different levels. The most common level is the physical, targeted in most forms of healthcare and therapy because physical substances, such as medications, affect the physical body. It also includes herbal remedies and many manipulative therapies such as massage and chiropractic. A key element is that all of these physical interventions can be extremely useful. Lives are saved every day by surgery, medicine and other therapies. They all improve health and wellbeing.

Certainly, the Physical Body can influence the higher levels. For instance, a change to the Physical Body can make the Vital Body feel healthier. It can change moods and emotions. It can even change attitudes in the Mental Body. However, these changes are limited. They are shifts that are not actually permanent. True healing occurs when there is a full paradigm shift, an "a ha" moment. That occurs when the knowledge and information on a subject are transformed into wisdom. That wisdom is the ultimate goal.

Once this paradigm shift has occurred, it is a permanent change. Shifts at the Physical Body level are really just first aid and this aspect needs to be realized. They will bring about other changes but those changes can be short-lived. I am sure you too, often find the need for repetition and maintenance in the use of physical therapies and medicine. In other words, adjustments have to be continued indefinitely or pills taken "for the rest of your life." Although surgery is more permanent, it is still an ongoing process. Remember, treatment at the Physical Body level does not flow up to bring about permanent changes because unless there are changes at the higher levels, nothing is going to cause a major shift that is permanent.

The Vital Body covers a lot of territory because that encompasses the world of energy medicine. Classical energy medicine includes acupuncture, shamanism, homeopathy, and Bach flower remedies, etc. In the foundation levels, BodyTalk works primarily on both the Physical Body and Vital Body levels. There are aspects of BodyTalk that are called energy medicine because the chakras, meridians, and energy fields are addressed as part of the formulas.

The Vital Body has an extra influence because the flow is downward. It means that when change occurs at the Vital Body level, the Physical Body is also affected in a very powerful way. It is likely that energy medicine will have a better and more lasting effect than strictly physical medicine. Often, if the two are combined, better results can be achieved. Affecting the Vital Body through energy medicine work is a superior system from the quantum physics point of view and from the model of the whole creative process.

The Mental Body is the realm of focusing on belief systems and attitudes that have developed. This includes the fields of psychology and psychotherapy – examining in depth why we are the way we are and understanding how much our belief systems, attitudes, and rigid rules for living have affected us.

Obviously, the Mental Body will have a profound effect and its bridging position midway on the ladder of Consciousness reflects this. As Dr. Bruce Lipton[21] elaborates in his work *The Biology of Belief*, a person's belief systems and attitudes have been shown to influence cellular function and, therefore, body chemistry and physiology. Belief systems have a flow-down effect from the Mental Body to the Vital Body and the Physical Body. Hence, therapies targeting the mental level, which include counseling, psychotherapy, and other techniques like BreakThrough (a very powerful method of gaining wisdom through understanding how belief systems and attitudes are developed and seeing the inherent flaws in them), have the potential to have a strong effect on these lower bodies. If a person has a major shift in an attitude or belief, it is inevitably going to affect the Vital Body and the Physical Body. BodyTalk practitioners have seen many examples of this. I have seen cases where a lung tumor and other serious illnesses cleared up after a week or two following a shift in a belief system.

In BodyTalk, a lot of work is done at the Mental Body level. Many of the techniques taught in The BodyTalk System™ are designed to help the Mental Body function well. Not only are beliefs and attitudes examined but practitioners even explore how to maximize the capabilities of the mind.

A technique I developed a number of years ago called "MindScape" was designed to train people to utilize their minds more effectively. It can be used to explore the psychology of the mind, to improve study or sports performance, and enhance intuitive and psychic abilities. BodyTalk practitioners are encouraged to use this technique to improve their intuitive ability to ask the Innate Wisdom what to do in a balancing session.

Many physically-based therapeutic interventions do not take into account the Mental Body and are unable to obtain sustained results. A shift rarely occurs in the Vital Body or Physical Body level that does not first happen at the Mental Body level.

At the Supramental Body level (or the super-mental intellect), the ability to produce results comes down to methodology of treatment. The BodyTalk System™ accesses this level as much as possible by developing the intuitive processes so that they go beyond the level of intuition obtained at the mental level. In time, the intuition becomes very accurate and very clear because practitioners are seeing and working with the big picture.

The training of BodyTalk practitioners exposes them to the philosophy, physics, chemistry, and psychology of how the body works and how all of these systems interact with one another. Most importantly, techniques that can access the quantum level of manifestation at the causal plane are used. In other words, the formulas used include such terms as Fragmentation, Defragmentation, Re-evaluation, Recontextualization, Integration, Tensegrity, Synchronization, and Communication.

By using all of those advanced terms and implanting them in formulas for the Mental Body to run, with the help of the Supramental intellect, the bodymind can be influenced so that it becomes aware of the evolution of the conflicts that are going on in the person, whether physical, mental, emotional, or environmental.

At this level, the history of the person is taken into consideration along with fetal life and even previous lives. The immediate environment of the client, other environmental systems, and the relationships with work and family are also taken into account. Allergens, electromagnetic frequencies, radio waves, radiation, and external inputs as well as the internal environment of the body and how it is working are embraced.

By utilizing the language and the laws of quantum mechanics, BodyTalk is able to work at the Supramental level. An advanced PaRama BodyTalk practitioner that is using advanced PaRama techniques is working at all four levels.

The Healing Nature of Intuition

CHAPTER ELEVEN

11

The essential theory behind Consciousness-based healthcare is that the manifesting process has within it an Innate Wisdom that in BodyTalk is referred to as "Universal Consciousness." The wisdom of this Consciousness is available to us, via intuition, provided we are open to receiving that wisdom and have developed techniques to establish reliability in the way we interpret the information received.

This chapter takes a more in-depth look at the way intuition is perceived. Later in the chapter, it will be clear that intuition is equated to the Supramental intellect, which is the localized or "personal" aspect of Universal Consciousness.

It is convenient to talk about training our intuition to be more reliable but strictly speaking we must realize that the intuition does not require training or developing in any way. The intuition is the highest level of wisdom we have access to and is always there for us. The so-called training is really the process of refining our sensitivity to the intuition so that we can access it in its native form without the conditioning and filters acquired during our lifetime.

This may seem pedantic but so often people wanting to develop their intuition are seduced by that very term "develop the intuition" to the point that they start believing it is the intuition that is being developed and not their ability to understand what their essential nature at the Supramental level is trying to communicate at all times.

To start exploring why we have such limited conscious awareness of our essential nature, we can start with our primary means of communication – the five senses.

The Five Senses

We experience the world via the medium of our senses. The most obvious of these are our normal senses that are clearly operating at all times to enable us to see, touch, smell, taste, and hear the world. They operate as an interface with manifestation by giving constant feedback for orientation within the body and surroundings. They are registered by the brain and considered a measurement of standard consensus reality. Because of this, they tend to dominate our experience of life because the "false ego" interprets information from normal senses as real.

In relation to the normal five senses there are three observations for consideration:

1. Reality is not experienced through the senses, only the brain's interpretation of it after it has happened.

2. The senses limit the range of information about reality to which humans have access.

3. The limited information received by the brain is distorted by the filters of each sense.

Normal Senses	Subtle Senses
Sounds	Thoughts
Sight	Visualization
Touch	Felt Sense
Taste	Sensory Response
Smell	Awareness

Each of the normal senses, however, has a subtle component that is potentially even more powerful when we talk about Consciousness-based living. The subtle senses enable our intuitive interface with manifestation. They give constant subtle feedback that is filtered through the subconscious mind. They are registered in the conscious mind with varying degrees of clarity, depending upon how strongly they are filtered by our belief systems and attitudes toward life. Unfortunately, they often dominate our experience of life and tend to be mistrusted when they prove to be inaccurate so much of the time.

The Subtle Senses

Sound

The most dominant of the subtle senses is the sense of sound which manifests as thoughts. We hear our thoughts in a subtle way. In the same way that normal sound enters the brain and is perceived within the Mind, so do our thoughts. Thoughts come from the Supramental mind and register in the conscious mind. When the Mind acts upon the thoughts, the brain carries out the appropriate action. The brain cannot create thoughts. Experience shows us that we essentially have no real control. We cannot create an original thought on demand and have virtually no say as to which thoughts come in at any given time. Thoughts are always intuitive in nature but the accumulated filters of our life cloud our interpretation of them. Unstructured or "nuisance" thoughts simply represent unstructured representations of intuitive processes much the same as daydreaming. Once structured, thoughts become one of the reliable messengers of the intuitive processes.

Sight

The subtle sense of sight uses visualization which is a function of the Mind. Research has shown that the brain cannot readily distinguish between what is visualized in the Mind and what is visualized externally. In other words, when we see a train external to our body a particular area of the brain lights up. Research has shown that when we visualize the train, or even daydream about a train, the same area of the brain lights up. When visualization is acted upon, the mind commands the brain to take the action.

In one of the most well-known studies on Creative Visualization in sports, Russian scientists[25] compared four groups of Olympic athletes in terms of their physical and mental training ratios:

- Group 1 received 100% physical training;
- Group 2 received 75% physical training with 25% mental training;
- Group 3 received 50% mental training with 50% physical training;
- Group 4 received 75% mental training with 25% physical training.

Group 4 had the best performance results, indicating that certain types of mental training, such as consciously invoking specific subjective states, can have significant measurable effects on biological performance. According to Cummins, "The Soviets had discovered that mental images can act as a prelude to muscular impulses."

Touch

All movement within our body or external to the body is registered by the Mind as a subtle felt sense of touch. Subtle touch gives us an awareness of our world at the deep intuitive level and registers in both the brain and Mind. This is also often referred to as our "felt sense" or a "knowing" of something. The concept of entanglement allows this "knowing" to operate at any distance limited only by the filters of our belief systems.

Taste and Smell

Taste and smell at the subtle level work very closely together. They are also a key part of general awareness of our body and environment. They are closely connected to the amygdala complex as part of our flight/fight response. They primarily register through the brain to be acknowledged by the Mind.

The subtle senses most often work together and it can be hard to discern exactly which subtle sense is being experienced at any given moment, whereas most people can clearly distinguish between seeing the wind blowing things around, feeling the wind on their body, and hearing the wind. With subtle senses, the practitioner may be drawn to an area of a person's body but unsure if it was a subtle sound (thought), subtle touch (felt sense or knowing), or subtle sight which drew their awareness there.

Universal Consciousness

The concept of dividing Consciousness up into several components appears redundant when considering that everything is Consciousness. However, in order to communicate effectively, it is sometimes necessary to make these divisions to clearly establish a definition for each term used. This is a broad philosophical subject and there is no exact right or wrong in the labels.

Universal Consciousness in the context of this book relates to the sum total of manifestation including the non-manifest. Remember that the physical world as perceived by the senses is still only a form of energy which, in turn, is a concept derived from observation through our normal and subtle senses.

Limitations of Mind Function

One of the interesting complexities of life is the way a series of beliefs, attitudes, and cultural indoctrinations are built up and stored in the mind/brain complex. The source of these can include inherited genetic tendencies, cultural and religious factors as well as life experiences including emotional, and environmental trauma.

This is the assortment of factors called "filters" for each lifetime. They profoundly influence the mind/brain interaction because all the information coming from the Supramental intellect, via the Mind, will be distorted in some way by these filters. In some cases, the filters may act in an apparently positive way but generally they tend to be disruptive.

This has significant influence on the subject of this chapter. Intuitive freedom of expression flowing from the Supramental intellect can be greatly inhibited by these filters. Some of the classic filters may be belief systems determining that good intuition is not yet developed and the information received cannot be trusted. Unfortunately, the reality is that this often appears true for most people.

This is why concrete steps must be taken to negate the influence of those filters by setting up the right parameters to bypass them. Regular clinical work is recommended to reduce the number of filters by learning to understand their etiology. The BodyTalk System™ includes the BreakThrough System, which is a very effective method of gaining a deeper understanding of how the filters develop, combined with effective tools for defusing them.

The BreakThrough System is a method of self-enquiry underpinned by the principles of Advaita. Students are given practical tools with which to hone the art of lateral thinking. Using deductive reasoning and guided by the intuitive processes, students journey into the paradoxical nature of conflict and the human psyche. The shifts in perspective that come from working with the BreakThrough principles transform programmed, reactionary living into a more conscious, fulfilling life.

Functioning Tools

It is important to summarize here that everything I am talking about has to do with various states of energy. Everything is energy. The objects that are seen are simply energy under observation which causes them to take on an appearance of solidity and specific function. However, much of the energy not seen also has the ability to function in an ordered way. This principle is used every day with electronics and most activities undertaken in this modern era.

Years of practical experience and experimentation have shown that non-visible energy can be influenced by the Mind using focusing tools and wisdom to create clear intent with attention. Once a clear understanding of what focusing tools can be utilized for any function to be achieved, then that knowledge, combined with wisdom, will give intent, focus and attention to the Mind that can bring about significant changes in all aspects of life. This is evidenced by the success rate of energy medicines such as acupuncture and BodyTalk.

Left and Right Brain

The concept of the left-brain tends to relate to the response of the brain to the normal senses. The right-brain concept relates more specifically to the subtle senses. Based on this postulate, the left-brain is more focused on the interpretation of the environmental stimuli as related to the normal senses whereas the right-brain is more closely aligned to the subtle senses and, therefore, more closely related to the Mind.

Imagination

Imagination includes the concepts of daydreaming, visualization, dreaming, and general thoughts and has several important functions which include:

- Exercise for the brain: The brain functions like muscle tissue. Muscle tissue can be built up with exercise. However, if exercising is stopped, the muscle tissue will start to break down again. Exercising the brain improves neural synapses and establishes more sophisticated neurological patterns to improve brain function. If the brain is not used then it will deteriorate. The process of daydreaming involves a very sophisticated neurological patterning that acts as excellent exercise for the brain.

- To process stress, the body also uses all the functions of imagination. Much of daydreaming, and dreaming, involves a symbolic processing of life activities through free association, and abstract symbolism.

- Extensive childhood daydreaming is a familiar trend in some of the biographies of the greatest minds in history. This appears to be evidence for increased development of the brain. Further, history shows that most new information and major discoveries tend to come through the processes involved with imagination.

> Researchers[26] have found a correlation between daydreaming and creativity – those who are more prone to mind-wandering tend to be better at generating new ideas.

Limitations of Imagination

The greatest limitation of the imagination process is that it is basically unstructured and can tend to be unreliable from the point of view of producing factual information that can be trusted without other methods of testing that information.

Intuition

By using thermography, Neurophysiology has established that imagination and intuition operate in the same regions of the brain and are led by active involvement of the Mind. The difference between daydreaming and intuition is significant - daydreaming is unstructured imagination, intuition is revealed through structured imagination.

Intuition is, by nature, reliable and accurate. The problem perceived with "faulty" intuition is because the filters do not allow the Mind to correctly interpret the wisdom of intuition.

Revealing Intuitive Information

The right-brain and Mind have the computing power and resources to create all aspects of imagination as tools to reveal intuition. Those resources include:

- subconscious (brain)
- Supramental consciousness (Mind and Innate Wisdom)
- accumulated wisdom – both individual and collective
- dharmic integrity (the Innate knowledge of "practical" living).

The left-brain gives structure to the imagination so that the Mind can perceive more clearly what is unstructured daydreaming and what is wisdom. Its resources include:

- accumulated knowledge
- trained skills
- learned procedures.

Contrary to popular opinion, the left-brain function is critical for the accurate perception of intuition which can be quite specific in its nature. General accuracy is quite rare because often the critical ingredients coming from the left-brain function determines the accuracy. This is why someone can be very accurate in medical intuition but not accurate when it comes to interpersonal matters or other aspects of human development and knowledge.

Left-brain development includes the following factors:

- general accumulated knowledge
- a protocol or framework
- specialized knowledge in the area to focus intuitive abilities
- specialized techniques to establish the appropriate parameters to create an environment for accurate intuition to emerge:
    - a) developing the yes/no response
    - b) MindScape
    - c) metaphysical focusing tools
    - d) mind discipline tools such as meditation.

It is also important to address the factors that help to reduce the impact of filters that cloud the wisdom of intuition:

- BreakThrough – addressing the limiting belief systems around the "perceived" inaccuracies of intuition

- extensive training involved with the utilization of the intuition along with stringent checks on the accuracy of results

- respecting the power of intuition by not using it inappropriately as a "party trick."

Left/Right Brain Integration

The intuition has a better chance of revealing its wisdom when the right-brain information coming in from the Supramental intellect is anchored and focused by developed left-brain structures.

The left-brain structures (protocols) will act as a focusing tool for the right-brain to clearly allow the wisdom of intuition to flow. The final degree of success of the outcome is also influenced by the integrity of the practitioner and a corresponding lack of agenda as to the nature of the information. (Being open to the "truth" rather than what our filters want to hear!)

Observation to Manifestation

It is important to note at this stage that when we are opening up to the intuitive process, we are also developing our intent, focus, and attention. Dr. Robert Lanza,[27] in his revolutionary book on Biocentrism, clearly summarizes the collective knowledge of quantum physics to show that our focus and intent is a key factor to observation, and resultant manifestation. This refers not only to the consensus reality we see, but also to the changes that can be made to that physical manifestation through focus on intuition. "Depending upon the actions of the observer," relates primarily to the focus, intent, and related clarity of the observer.

For years scientists have been causing wave functions to collapse, subjecting them to stringent limitations within scientific experiments. Eventually, it became obvious that the mere knowledge in the experimenter's mind of what they wanted done was sufficient to cause the wave function to collapse into a specific result.[27] It was obvious in these experiments that the experimenter had sufficient left-brain knowledge, coupled with right-brain consciousness, to bring about the changes. In other words, untrained or unskilled people will not get the same effect because they do not have the same trained focus of left- and right-brained information coalescing to create the desired result. This marriage of the left- and right-brain in this focused way is the basis of Consciousness-based science.

Science has repeatedly shown that the intent of the experimenter is sufficient to change the world seen "out there." In other words, what is happening in our minds actually determines what is happening "out there." Even more importantly, everything happens instantaneously, no matter what the perceived distance from us. I should point out that all this theory is straight out of classical quantum physics textbooks!

Mental "Scaffolding"

Until the Mind and left-brain actually lay down the conceptual framework (scaffolding) to cause differentiation in the haze of probabilities that represent the object's range of possible values, the object cannot be thought of as being either here or there.

The famous Copenhagen interpretation of quantum theory was deduced by the three greatest scientific minds of their time: Albert Einstein, Niels Bohr, and Werner Heisenberg. The conclusion was the realization that nothing is real unless it is perceived.

Awareness, Focus, Attention and Observation

Up to this point the focus has been on the usefulness of accessing the wisdom of intuition in solving many of the mysteries of life and giving greater understanding of what is happening within, for example, a sick body. This is extremely useful and has unlimited application across the full spectrum of human experience.

Stages of Healing

In the first stages of healing as practised in the early courses of BodyTalk, and many other healing modalities, a perceived separation exists between the intuitive process that gives rise to solutions for certain health challenges and the techniques or formulas indicated to bring about the appropriate changes.

At this stage, the left/right brain intuitive process sets up the mental scaffolding that will enable a formula to be collapsed through the observation of a practitioner.

In this case, the intuitive process appears to serve several functions:

- provides information of what needs to be addressed
- establishes the techniques and formula necessary to bring about the appropriate change
- provides focus, attention and intent for the technical formula to be implemented.

This stage of healing perceives intuition as a source of information and guidance in order to facilitate a more conscious approach to implementing healing techniques. Science is clearly saying otherwise. I will now look at the true implications of what has been discussed so far in this chapter.

The Healing Nature of Intuition

At this point, it should be clear that access to accurate intuitive wisdom is intimately involved with clear focus, attention and intent that then gives rise to observation. This logically means that intuitive wisdom does not just give the ability to understand what is necessary to solve problems such as health problems. It also gives the energy matrix a clear understanding of the etiology of the problem. This in turn will become an observation that will give rise to tangible physical changes within the structures observed.

When describing a purely quantum or holistic phenomenon it must be realized that the intuitive act of observing has also become the practical means of treatment and healthcare.

The BodyTalk System™ embraces the understanding that the dynamic relationship between the patient and the practitioner gives rise to a quantum entanglement where the problem and the solution can coexist as part of the same process.

In the advanced levels of BodyTalk, intuition is being acknowledged as both the source of understanding disease and the instrument through which deep levels of healing occur. This reinforces the famous philosophical statement, "Understanding is all."

The advanced formulas of BodyTalk that I talk about in this book give descriptions of the processes that enable the healing to occur. They are not prescriptions to make the healing occur. The healing process utilizes the presence and therapeutic entanglement of the practitioner and patient. However, the practitioner is acting as a facilitator – not a healer.

When the practitioner truly understands the nature of intuition operating at this level, spontaneous healing can easily occur. Intuition does not know the boundaries of space and time. In these situations, major physical changes such as the disappearance of tumors, or a total repair of a hole in the heart while the patient is still lying on the treatment table, may be seen.

While the practitioner continues to indulge the concept of using formulas and techniques to facilitate the healing process then the process that occurs will be happening in the space/time continuum. In other words, the healing process will take the time that the practitioner's limited ego-based belief systems expect it to take!

This does not mean formulas and techniques should not be used. They act as focusing tools and provide credibility for the limited understanding of the patient. Also, by describing the process that intuition is using, the utilization of the formula enhances the focusing, attention, and intent involved in the healing dynamic. The key here is to use the appropriate focusing tools while still maintaining a deeper understanding of the true nature of healing.

A deep understanding of the scientific and philosophical theories outlined in this chapter and utilized in advanced BodyTalk can free us from the limitations of centuries of conditioned thinking and limited Cartesian approaches to healing processes.

Advanced Techniques – CDRRII

CHAPTER TWELVE

12

One of the advanced BodyTalk procedures frequently used in sessions by PaRama practitioners is the CDRRII formula (pronounced ceedree). Each letter of the formula represents a procedural step as follows:

C: Circulation Plug-in
D: Differentiate
    Defragment (defrag)
    Fragment
R: Re-contextualize
R: Re-evaluate
I: Integrate
I: Introspect

The foregoing quantum scientific principles are one of the cornerstones of the training and education process for all BodyTalk practitioners. All PaRama BodyTalk practitioners understand that the role they play in the healing process is that of catalyst, not cause or "healer." Working within the framework of The BodyTalk System™ protocols, the BodyTalk practitioner draws on their deep understanding of the various levels, systems, and dynamics that constitute the bodymind.

Practising from this place of skill combined with objectivity, the practitioner has clarity of attention, which gives rise to focused observation. This combination of objective focus and non-involvement with outcome, allows the BodyTalk techniques to effectively catalyze change in the energy balance of the bodymind. The subsequent change in the energy blueprint will alter the structure of the cells of the body which in turn will bring about transformation of the physiology at all levels.

Circulation Plug-In

At the physical level, it is well established that the body parts undergoing repair require good blood supply to, from, and within the relevant part of the body. Similarly, these body parts also need adequate nerve supply and lymph flow. In addition, the mental and energy bodies have their own circulation requirements. These circulatory needs will include the free flow of energy to the area via the acupuncture meridians, chakras and nadis, consciousness, electrons, protons, and electromagnetic frequencies.

In acute situations such as an injury, the full circulation of all the aforementioned factors tends to take place naturally. However, many people are still slow in the healing of acute injuries because these circulations do not flow as well as they could. This circulatory deficiency is the result of the various stress factors and habits that the body has been, or is, dealing with.

In chronic situations, many aspects of these circulatory requirements are not flowing to the site of imbalance, injury, or disease. This inhibition of the circulatory systems not only slows down the recovery process but can even bring the healing process to a halt, leaving the body in a chronic, unhealthy state.

By directing the pre-frontal cortex with the Circulation Plug-in, the healing process of acute injuries is accelerated and rapid healing in chronic situations is activated. Hence, the Circulation Plug-in is utilized in virtually every advanced formula in BodyTalk.

Differentiate

Defragmentation

Amazingly, a computer can greatly mimic the functioning of the human body. As discovered in Biophysics, the storage of information in the connective tissue of the body tends to occur as a binary function of on/off switches at the atomic level, which is the same storage function as a computer hard drive. BodyTalk practitioners know from clinical results that the pre-frontal cortex of the brain can be set up to run programs, similar to computer programs, which have a very distinct effect on the functioning of the body. A good example is the Defragmentation program.

When using a computer, how often does the machine slow down and seem to be getting slower and slower when opening a file or program? We start thinking we have to purchase a new computer, until someone comes along (usually a child) and asks, "Have you defragged your computer?" First we must know that a defragmentation program exists! We then run the defragmentation program on the computer, which sorts out all of the files that have become fragmented, and suddenly the computer runs a great deal faster. A simple process has saved the cost of buying a new computer.

All stressors contribute to the fragmentation of bodily functions particularly those of the brain and the nervous system. The autonomic functions of the body to do with digestion, hormonal balance, posture, and coordination all rely on coordination patterns held in the nervous and energic systems. This also includes the database of the immune system and short- and long-term memory.

All these functions are held as functional morphogenic fields so that every activity does not have to be relearned each time the particular skill is required. These fields are prone to corruption and fragmentation by various stress factors. The deterioration of certain skills, or even their complete loss after trauma, can cause major disruption in the body.

The BodyTalk System™ has demonstrated that the Innate Wisdom can help locate the functions that are fragmented and then have the pre-frontal cortex run a Defragmentation program to correct the problem. This program will work on physical structures, such as connective tissue information storage, as well as the energic blueprint of the body. Energy field function can be defragged and restored within a few minutes. In the case of the connective tissue, which is analogous to the hard drive, the program may take a day or two before noticeable change occurs.

The changes can be profound. An important example lies in coordination programs – the way in which virtually all coordination skills are learned, from the simple ones like walking to the more complex, detailed skills used by a gifted craftsman or athlete. An illustration of an advanced coordination skill is a baseball pitcher's repertoire of different pitches: each pitch requires an entirely different coordination of his arm, fingers, and movement of the body.

Many people find that their coordination functions have been compromised following an event, trauma, surgery, or accident or have simply deteriorated over time. In BodyTalk, once the Innate Wisdom has identified the particular problem, the Defragmentation program is run to restore that function. This process has tremendous application.

Case Study

An excellent example of this involved a 22-year-old baseball pitcher who required a rotator cuff repair of his shoulder. He was playing in the minor leagues with aspirations of being called up to the major leagues. Following surgery, he participated in rehabilitation but six months post-surgery, he discovered he had lost his coordination for his slider pitch. He simply could not throw this pitch at all yet the other three pitches were intact. This was a tremendous disappointment especially in the context of his aspiration to be called up to the major leagues.

In the BodyTalk session, I established that during the perioperative period, the coordination pattern for this pitch was fragmented at both the energy blueprint level and the functional level between the cerebellum and basal ganglion. The Defragmentation program on this coordination pattern took only a few minutes to run. After it finished, the young man was told to throw his pitches. He threw a couple of the ordinary pitches first and then he found he threw the slider pitch perfectly. He had no problems throwing the slider pitch after that. He did not have to retrain himself from the beginning again. The functioning of the coordination pattern, whose breakdown had led to the ineffectiveness of executing that particular pitch, just needed to be restored.

In BodyTalk, this can be done for many different skills. Sometimes basketball players, over a period of time through general injury, emotional stressors, and traumas, will gradually lose their three-point shooting ability or their free-throw shooting ability. Their coordination pattern seems lost. They try to persevere with that pattern rather than re-establish a new one. This leads to gradual further deterioration of that skill and in turn, their career. By running the Defragmentation program on that area and restoring function, the coordination matrix starts to work properly again, the basketball player's game improves, and his career is revived.

This applies to any form of sport or any developed set of skills that people have, even the basic ones. A person having a hip replacement, or any other joint replacement, needs to return quickly to the activities of daily living. The actual surgery and the complete change of angles mean that the old coordination patterns are quite ineffective and they are invariably disrupted. In relearning new patterns, the old ones keep interfering and slow down the rehabilitation. Over time, physical therapists are able to help the patient regain functional coordination skills.

In BodyTalk, the rehabilitation process can be accelerated by defragmenting the original walking pattern. This gives patients a head start and re-establishes a basic coordination pattern. The physical therapy then modifies and fine-tunes rehabilitation to compensate for the change in the angle of their gait because of the prosthetic replacement. The whole rehabilitation process is sped up. The application of BodyTalk in rehabilitation can have truly extraordinary results.

Another major use of the Defragmentation program is in the rehabilitation of stroke victims. BodyTalk practitioners have found that even in people who have suffered a stroke several years previously and lost the use of a hand, the use of BodyTalk techniques can repair the lesions of the brain caused by the stroke. The neurological supply then returns to the hand and the hand demonstrates movement again. What can slow the rehabilitation process in restoring the fine motor skills of the hand is the fact that the coordination matrix has deteriorated. So in addition to clearing the scar tissue and repairing the motor segment of the brain, the coordination matrix for the hand is defragmented.

A rather surprising application of the Defragmentation technique is in general brain function where the person may be a mathematician, scholar, or have other mental skills. Such skills can gradually be eroded for the same reasons as motor skills. The brain loses the ability to easily do calculations or perform the academic thinking it previously did with ease. Mathematics and language involve access to memory patterns that are in good order. Once again, running the Defragmentation program on the affected parts of the brain connected to the skills that have degenerated will restore those functions.

I am very excited about this particular technique, which is used in conjunction with other techniques in the advanced levels of BodyTalk. Defragmentation is so simple to actually run and perform, and results are rapid and significant.

Fragmentation

Scars, adhesions, lesions, and small tumors on the skin or in the body have long been recognized as a major health problem. You will recall from the section on Scars that the disruption due to a lack of energy flow played a significant role in various health conditions, particularly if it was located across a meridian or right on an acupuncture point.

While the Scars technique works well for external scars, internal scars can be a major problem in patient healthcare. These include adhesions as a result of injuries or operations, and lesions formed as a result of internal bleeding or hemorrhaging. Internal scars greatly interfere with the flow of energy and communication along the connective tissues and impede the flow of electrons in the same way that an obstruction in a garden hose prevents the flow of water. Blockages due to long-term adhesions and lesions interfere with the functioning of the whole human body. Addressing these blockages must become a priority.

Using advanced BodyTalk formulas these internal scars can now be broken up. This technique is based on the ability of the brain to utilize formulas that will run a program to specifically address the scarring. One of these programs is the Fragmentation program. This, again, is a very simple technique used by PaRama BodyTalk practitioners.

At this stage there has been insufficient research to demonstrate exactly how the body is actually executing the fragmentation. So far, the focus has been on the clinical results, with MRI reports showing that lesions, adhesions and even tumors have cleared in various parts of the body, including the brain.

The concept is that the pre-frontal cortex is programmed to set up conditions that will bombard the lesions, scar tissue, or small tumors with protons or neutrons. This is actually quite similar to the latest machines used in treating tumors in cancer that fire protons or neutrons at them to break them up. It is likely that this is the same process that the body is doing when programmed by a PaRama BodyTalk practitioner.

In a case study with benign tumors in the brain that were affecting brain function, surgery was the suggested and encouraged medical option, even though the tumors were not malignant. The Fragmentation program was implemented for the tumors, along with the Circulation Plug-in technique to increase lymph and blood flow to remove the particles that broke away as the lesion was breaking up. The tumors disappeared in a matter of a few days. This result has been confirmed clinically through repeated MRI scans that showed the tumors no longer existed.

This aspect of BodyTalk is very important. Throughout a given lifetime injuries to the head may be received resulting in minor or major concussions. With such injuries blood vessels will rupture and form lesions which gradually build up in the brain and reduce its functioning. The deterioration of brain function and memory as humans get older is clinically shown to result from an accumulation of lesions in the brain. The Fragmentation program is designed to work through the brain clearing these lesions resulting in tremendous reversal of deterioration of the brain to the point that people are getting their memories back, they are thinking more clearly and feeling happier as a result.

Athletes who have received many head injuries often demonstrate major illness later in life. Another major incidence showing up now is the many disorders found among soldiers who have brain damage from explosions. This is an important area where the new technology of BodyTalk would make a huge difference in the wellbeing and recovery of both athletes and soldiers resulting in immense savings in long-term traditional healthcare.

Stroke is another challenge where lesions to the brain can often cause severe brain damage. Again, there are many case studies in BodyTalk involving people who had suffered a stroke more than 10 years previously, causing loss of virtually all function of one hand. The lesions were cleared in the motor cortex and cerebellum of the brain, using this Fragmentation technique. After just a few weeks of BodyTalk sessions, use of the hand had been regained. Then with the appropriate physical therapy to regenerate the hand function and the muscles, normal hand function resumed within a few months. This approach works particularly well when combined with the Defragmentation technique described in the previous section.

Obviously, this is another very exciting aspect of BodyTalk. The Differentiation techniques can play a huge role in healthcare in general, particularly after surgery or other procedures. In many cases of surgery the problems afterwards often stem from the formation of internal scars, lesions, and adhesions that cause discomfort to the person. Healthcare practitioners can run these programs after an operation to ensure these negative effects do not occur. This approach will improve both the quality and speed of the rehabilitation process.

Re-contextualization, Re-evaluation, Integration and Introspection

Most health imbalances have a history of stress-related factors. These stressors will have compromised the effective functioning of the various physiological systems that are imperative for good health. When any one of them is compromised, the relationship between the various systems becomes dysfunctional. Consequently, coordination of all the body's healthy physiological and biochemical resources is disrupted and poor health ensues. The PaRama BodyTalk principles of Re-contextualization, Re-evaluation, Integration and Introspection effectively address such disruptions.

Part of the healing process is for the various aspects of the systemic disruption to be brought into perspective, reorganized, and put into the correct context. The word re-contextualize comes from the Latin "contestus" which means, "to weave together."

How re-contextualization pertains to BodyTalk is that it involves the weaving together of all the correct associations required. As was addressed in earlier chapters, health imbalances can involve relationships to the total environment of the patient. These relationships include the internal workings of the body as well as all the physical, emotional, and energic environmental associations. These situations need to be re-contextualized and placed in the right perspective for healing to occur.

Once the functioning of the system has been re-contextualized, all the systemic relationships need to be re-evaluated. Re-evaluation here means "juxtapose Cartesian relationships." In other words, the body needs to prioritize the causative factors as they relate to the symptoms of the disease. The re-evaluation could also involve re-assessing how to achieve the optimum balance in an area of the patient's body or environment and assessing what change is needed.

The word priority comes up all the time in BodyTalk. This is because prioritization is one of the major philosophical differences between The BodyTalk System™ and other healthcare systems. Prioritizing ensures that the factors in need of attention are being addressed in the right sequence. Furthermore, this re-evaluation through prioritization is established and put into effect by the Innate Wisdom of the body - not the practitioner.

Through the quantum approach, Re-contextualization and Re-evaluation are guided by intuition via the pre-frontal cortex. The BodyTalk protocol serves as a framework within which the intuitive processes of the practitioner can effectively establish the priorities within the bodymind. In this way, the patient's body is being trained to start functioning as it is intended.

Quantum theory demonstrates that a significant problem in healthcare in general is that the Cartesian approach often fails to address the big picture. The Cartesian approach is antithetical to our present-day understanding of the essential, holistic nature of manifestation. This big picture perspective in healthcare involves the recognition that all interactions have to be well coordinated and well organized. For optimum health recovery to occur, all systemic interactions have to transpire within the right context, be re-evaluated according to priorities, and then integrated within the system.

Subsequent to effecting Re-contextualization and Re-evaluation within the system, it is crucial to set in motion the process of Integration. The Integration process ensures that all the changes that have occurred within the organ, body part, or physiological system are reflected in the bigger picture of the body as a whole. Integration also ensures that change effected in any single aspect of the body is also reflected within all other aspects of the bodymind complex. By means of the process of Integration, the PaRama BodyTalk practitioner is able to catalyze dramatic changes in the functioning and coordination of all systems within the body. When this systemic transformation occurs, the bodymind as a whole can operate more efficiently. Another way of saying this is that the body has shifted from a Cartesian way of functioning to holistic quantum functioning.

The final stage of the CDRRII formula is the process of Introspection. The understanding taught in The BodyTalk System™ is that all changes made to the bodymind need to be sent to the heart-brain complex for storage. This part of the formula is a more specific version of tapping the heart to store the changes described in the earlier chapters. In this case, the large amount of specific information that has been generated through the CDRRII formula is specifically encoded into the consciousness of the heart-brain.

Search and Retrieve (SR)

CHAPTER THIRTEEN

13

When addressing the health challenges of a specific organ, body part, or system, the formula has to be specific. It is vital that the formula used takes into account the etiological stress factors that led to the disruption of function. The earlier chapters on the basic techniques of BodyTalk showed how these etiological factors could be addressed by targeting individual situations such as active memories, past biochemical stress factors, or environmental factors.

The basic techniques of The BodyTalk System™ can and do achieve excellent results in the average situation. However, in more complex cases, a sophisticated approach needs to be taken. This is where the PaRama BodyTalk Search and Retrieve (SR) formula comes into play.

For example, the PaRama BodyTalk practitioner may be addressing the liver function of a patient which has been compromised through a lifetime of stresses. Some of these stresses may be active memories involving traumatic situations in the patient's history. These stresses brought about pathological change within the liver and continue to contribute to its malfunctioning. Instead of addressing individual active memories, "threads" of incidences are searched for in the advanced SR technique.

Observation has shown that early childhood emotional traumas are interpreted by the mind and imprinted within the psyche in the form of belief systems and attitudes. These interpretations can be summed up as a hierarchy of projected assumptions about self and life. These assumptions distort our experience of life until they are put into perspective. The powers of projection of the psyche will continue to manifest situations over many years that have a similar emotional pattern. For example, early childhood abuse can set in motion a lifelong history of abusive situations, leading to frustration, anger, and a victim consciousness that can greatly compromise the liver function.

By intuitively establishing the early childhood theme of the emotional thread, the SR formula will then take into account all the associated stored active memories right up to the present time. The SR formula will then run a series of dynamic parallel active memory techniques (as described in Chapter 6), which will interact with each other and diffuse the stressful holding patterns in the cells as well as supply the wisdom gained through this process.

All this information will then be integrated into the CDRRII formula as it is running. Similar threads can be established for environmental factors and any biochemical issues such as toxins, heavy metal poisoning, and allergy reactions.

Summary and Conclusion

CHAPTER FOURTEEN

The BodyTalk System™ has pioneered the understanding that the Innate Wisdom of the body has access to all the knowledge and resources to bring about changes at the cellular level. Further, once it is given the right directions, the pre-frontal cortex of the patient can run programs to facilitate the appropriate changes throughout the body. This new approach to the biophysics of the bodymind represents a major breakthrough in healthcare. When given clarity the body can, and will, heal itself in most situations.

In my experience The BodyTalk System™ is the only new health care system in the world that actually attempts to work on all of the levels and obey many of the laws of quantum physics. This is not by accident. It is because quantum physics and, in particular, the dynamic systems theory, was always my favorite subject and I also looked at all of the different healthcare systems when designing the techniques in BodyTalk. Because of this design, I can confidently say, BodyTalk is Consciousness-based. Working at the Supramental Body level, the higher levels of Consciousness are accessed. Consciousness is consulted on how to address the needs of the client so that the exact formula can be created that is going to bring about a causal shift and in turn, cascade down to the other three levels.

Dr. Goswami is referred to as "The Quantum Activist" because he is actively trying to show how quantum theory should be applied to economics, politics, environmental controls, and every aspect of life. Unless the true nature of manifestation is understood, the impact is limited to working at the physical level only. Any practitioner or therapist may have very good intentions in healthcare, the environment, or any other aspect of life but good intentions do not necessarily get good results. Wisdom, focus and attention, and the understanding of how evolution is actually occurring, are also needed. The BodyTalk System™ is poised to deepen the understanding of the working of Consciousness through the bodymind. The implications for the future of healthcare are vast and truly exciting.

This is the medicine of the future. All those involved in The BodyTalk System™ are proud to say that BodyTalk is a Consciousness-based healthcare system. What we hope is that, eventually, all healthcare systems will incorporate an understanding of the science of the body from a quantum point of view. This greater depth of understanding of the bodymind will undoubtedly enhance the work of any practitioner.

BodyTalk in the Future

We live in exponential times. Technological and scientific advances are transforming the way we experience our world so quickly that it is impossible to foresee even a few years ahead with any accuracy. What is known, however, is that no matter how much these changes might simplify and improve our lives, their magnitude has the potential of bringing untold added stressors that will impact our health globally.

Until now it might have seemed to you that healthcare lags in comparison to the phenomenal advances being made in technology. But, hopefully, this book has given you reason to pause. I have only touched on some of the very basic concepts of The BodyTalk System™, but sufficiently I think, to give you a sense of its current and potential scope of practice.

As you might now understand, The BodyTalk System™ is a complete healthcare profession in its own right. The BodyTalk Protocol and Procedures ensure that the priorities of the bodymind are respected and that all the healthcare issues it is capable of resolving are addressed effectively. Simultaneously, the Protocol ensures that we engage other healthcare systems where appropriate. There will always be a need for good rehabilitation programs such as physical therapy and occupational therapy. There will always be a need for surgery and pharmacological intervention when a condition becomes so severe that the body is incapable of healing itself by natural methods. Psychological counseling, contemplative practices, and nutrition are other obvious important, indispensable areas of the healthcare system.

I feel that the biggest asset of The BodyTalk System™ is that it follows the natural laws of manifestation. BodyTalk will always look at the relationships and communication between all the body parts that are necessary for empowered healthy living. Coupled with this, other relationships of the bodymind are explored, together with all aspects of the environment and the personal history of the patient. This is why The BodyTalk System™ is called a holistic and integrated system of healthcare. BodyTalk is very much a system of preventative health maintenance rather than a system of first aid for acute conditions.

The PaRama BodyTalk levels bring forth the principles of quantum theory and biophysics so that the complexities of more serious health challenges can also be addressed in a natural way. The use of the advanced intuitive process enables PaRama BodyTalk practitioners to explore realms of wellbeing far beyond the normal process of treating current symptoms.

The principles and practice of The BodyTalk System™ are still in the stage of rapid development. The basic BodyTalk System can be learned as a standalone profession. However, one of the most exciting aspects of BodyTalk that is happening right now, and will continue to happen exponentially, is the integration of the BodyTalk principles into all other healthcare systems. There is an increasing amount of specialization within the BodyTalk profession that is utilizing the best of what the entire medical model has to offer.

The basic techniques of BodyTalk – such as BodyTalk Access – are being utilized in schools, work environments, home environments, and among indigenous people throughout the world. This aspect of BodyTalk not only improves the general wellbeing of the people involved but also helps them to function at their highest potential.

The International BodyTalk Association has established standards of practice for BodyTalk that involve the passing of exams, supervised practicals, and continuing education requirements. Although many thousands of people have learned BodyTalk, not all of these people have gone on to take the appropriate exams and participate in the continuing-education programs. It should be noted here that because The BodyTalk System™ teaches many subjects that help in understanding the life processes, there are many students with already-established careers. These students study BodyTalk purely for their own personal development and spiritual growth.

Should you wish to receive BodyTalk sessions, you are encouraged to consult the practitioner listings on the IBA website to ensure that you choose a Certified BodyTalk Practitioner who meets the standard requirements of The BodyTalk System™. There are geographical search tools incorporated into our listings so that you can quickly find the nearest qualified practitioners.

Thank you for taking this journey with me into the process of holistic integrative medicine. Should this book inspire you to learn more about BodyTalk, or to receive BodyTalk sessions, I invite you to visit our website: www.bodytalksystem.com. On the website, you will see many more articles, case studies, videos, and general information.

References

1. Sheldrake R. *The Presence of the Past: Morphic Resonance and the Habits of Nature.* London, UK: Collins; 1988:112.

2. Capra F. *The Turning Point: Science, Society, and the Rising Culture.* New York, NY: Simon and Schuster; 1982.

3. Grof S. *Beyond the Brain: Birth, Death and Transcendence in Psychotherapy.* Albany, NY: State University of New York; 1985:6.

4. Hoyle F. *The Intelligent Universe.* London: Michael Joseph; 1983:18-19.

5. Oschman J. *Energy Medicine: The Scientific Basis.* Edinburgh, UK: Churchill Livingstone/Harcourt Brace; 2000.

6. Goswami A. *The Quantum Doctor: A Physicist's Guide to Health and Healing.* Charlottesville, VA: Hampton Roads Publishing Company; 2004.

7. Balsekar R. About Ramesh. Ramesh Balsekar Official Website. http://www.rameshbalsekar.com/about.asp. Accessed October 19, 2012.

8. Hamilton C. Scientific Proof of the Existence of God: An interview with Amit Goswami. *What Is Enlightenment? Magazine.* Spring-Summer 1997.

9. Ventegodt S, Merrick J. What is consciousness? *J Altern Med Res.* 2011;3(3):285-287.

10. McCraty R. *Energetic Heart: Bioelectromagnetic Communication Within and Between People.* Boulder Creek, CA:Institute of Heart Math; 2003. http://www.ssporer.com/downloads/Energetic_Heart.pdf. Accessed October 19, 2012.

11. Latta, S. Hitting "The Wall". *Marathon and Beyond.* http://www.marathonandbeyond.com/choices/latta.htm. Updated September 2003. Accessed October 30th 2012.

12. Illumination Lighting. Wikipedia. http://en.wikipedia.org/wiki/Over-illumination. Updated October 12, 2012. Accessed October 19, 2012.

13. Batmanghelidj F. *Your Body's Many Cries for Water.* Vienna, VA: Global Health Solutions; 1997.

14. Steenhuysen J. Saliva nothing to spit at. *Globe and Mail.* March 25, 2008. http://www.theglobeandmail.com/technology/science/saliva-nothing-to-spit-at/article1053624/. Accessed October 15, 2012.

15. Smith S. Toxic chemicals finding their way into the womb. *CNN Health.* July 28, 2010. http://www.cnn.com/2010/HEALTH/06/01/backpack.cord.blood/index.html. Accessed October 15, 2012.

16. Candace P. Molecules of Emotion: The Science Behind Mind-Body Medicine. New York, NY: Touchstone; 1999.

17. Levin SM. The Tensegrity-Truss as a Model for Spine Mechanics: Biotensegrity. *J Mech in Med and Biol.* 2002;2(3&4):375-388.

18. Flemons T. The Bones of Tensegrity. Intension Designs. http://www.intensiondesigns.com/bones_of_tensegrity.html. Access October 16, 2012.

19. The Ghost in your Genes. BBC-Science and Nature-Horizon. January 2006. http://www.bbc.co.uk/sn/tvradio/programmes/horizon/ghostgenes.shtml. Accessed October 15, 2012.

20. Carl G. Jung Quotes on Astrology. Astrology Weekly. http://www.astrologyweekly.com/astrology-articles/carl-g-jung-quotes.php. Accessed October 19, 2012.

21. Lipton BH. The Biology of Belief: Unleashing the Power of Consciousness, Matter & Miracles. United States: Hay House; 2008.

22. Science of the Heart: Exploring the Role of the Heart in Human Performance. Insitute of HeartMath. http://www.heartmath.org/research/science-of-the-heart/introduction.html. Accessed October, 16 2012.

23. Amoroso RL. *Complementarity of Mind and Body: Realizing the Dream of Descartes, Einstein, and Eccles.* Hauppauge, NY: Nova Science Publishers; 2010.

24. Crick FC, Kock C. What is the function of the claustrum? *Phil. Trans. R. Soc. B.* 2005;360:1271–1279. http://www.klab.caltech.edu/news/crick-koch-05.pdf. Accessed October 16, 2012.

25. Cummins W, Scaglione R. *Karate of Okinawa: Building Warrior Spirit.* New York, NY: Person-to-Person Publishing; 1994.

26. Lehrer J. The Virtues of Daydreaming. *The New Yorker.* June 5, 2012 http://www.newyorker.com/online/blogs/frontal-cortex/2012/06/the-virtues-of-daydreaming.html#ixzz1xc7EhoYV. Accessed October 16, 2012.

27. Lanza R, Berman B. *Biocentrism: How Life and Consciousness are the Keys to Understanding the True Nature of the Universe.* Dallas TX: Benbella Books; 2009.

Appendix A
Scientific Explanation

BY JAMES OSCHMAN, Ph.D.

Here, I discuss what BodyTalk and quantum physics can teach the physiologist, biophysicist, psychologist, physicist, physician and anyone else interested in the advancement of science and medicine; the contribution BodyTalk can make to the public welfare, and how BodyTalk can benefit our collective future.

When discoveries are made in physics, it is usually not long before medicine attempts to use them to create new tools for diagnosis or treatment. Examples include the discovery of electricity (Galvani), X-rays (Roentgen), magnetic resonance imaging (Damadian), and biophotons (Popp, Van Wijk, Bischof, and others). An exception is the discovery of the quantum.

The quantum story began at a specific moment, in the year 1900, when Max Planck reluctantly described his findings from the study of an obscure physical phenomenon known as black-body radiation in a presentation to the German Physical Society.[1] Planck's reluctance came from his realization that from that moment forward, the world of physics would never be the same. Planck's discovery: the energies found in nature do not behave the way everyone thought they did. The emissions of energy at different frequencies, as from a heated object, do not follow a smooth curve but come in discrete steps or jumps known as quanta.

Max Planck was correct. The world of physics would never be the same. All of this happened because the younger Max Planck did not heed the advice of a famous physicist who told him he should become a pianist rather than a physicist because physics was a finished and closed subject to which nothing new could be added.

It took a quarter of a century for Planck's discoveries to gel into a new branch of science we now know as quantum physics. Let us briefly summarize the history of this subject. The reader needs to know that we will be returning to most of these discoveries as we discuss the quantum aspects of BodyTalk. These discoveries are:

– Matter can be described as being composed of either particles or waves (French physicist Louis de Broglie in 1924).

– Matrix mechanics (German physicists Werner Heisenberg and Max Born in 1925).

– Wave mechanics and the non-relativistic Schrödinger equation as an approximation that could be used to apply de Broglie's theory by providing a "wave function" – a probability for the existence of a particle or a wave with a particular location and velocity (Austrian physicist Erwin Schrödinger in 1925).

– The uncertainty principle and the recognition that the observer is always a part of the experiment (Heisenberg in 1927).

– The Copenhagen interpretation of quantum mechanics - quantum mechanics does not describe an objective reality but deals only with probabilities of observing, or measuring, various aspects of reality (beginning around 1927). According to the Copenhagen interpretation, the act of observation or measurement causes the set of probabilities or possibilities to immediately and randomly assume only one of many possible values. This is called the collapse of the wave function. This aspect is especially important in the exploration of BodyTalk.

The unification of quantum mechanics with special relativity by proposing electron spin (a property of profound importance, as we shall see shortly) and the existence of the positron is an important start. Starting in 1927, Paul Dirac described the properties of "empty" space as a sea of energy created by the formation and disappearance of energetic particles – the Dirac Sea. A variety of other names have been given to empty space: the ether, the quantum vacuum, the quantum plenum, etc. (Figure 2) In essence, electrons and positrons bubble up from the quantum vacuum and then annihilate each other. While all of this activity cancels out to zero, and it appears that a sum total of nothing is happening, there is enormous potential for the storage of information and the production of matter and energy in the quantum dance.

During the same period, the Hungarian, John von Neumann, formulated a rigorous mathematical basis for quantum mechanics.

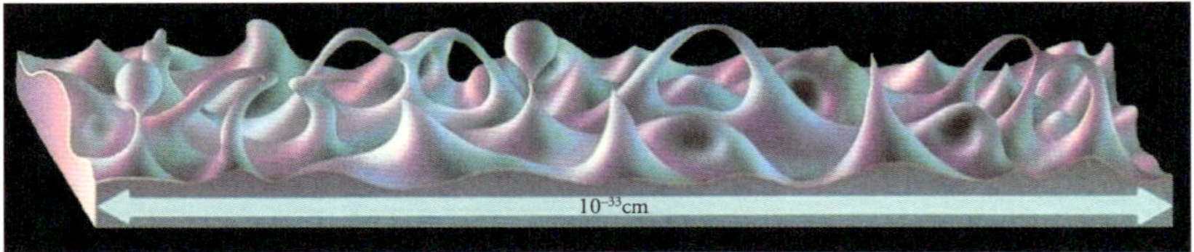

Figure 2: The Dirac Sea, ether, quantum vacuum, quantum plenum, etc., viewed at the smallest scale possible, known as the Planck length.

These discoveries, like many other works from the founding period of quantum physics, still stand and remain widely used. Of course, each aspect of the quantum world continues to be discussed and debated and one can say that there is no universal consensus among researchers. This means that someone somewhere will criticize any aspect of quantum physics we discuss here. While this might cause some scholars to hesitate to discuss these matters, there is a solution to the problem. It is said that the proof is in the pudding, and the proof of quantum concepts can be found in the technological successes of quantum electronics and in the therapeutic successes of quantum BodyTalk.

Quantum electronics has led to the development of extraordinary devices we use every day. Careful study of these technologies is of interest to the biophysicist who continually searches for clues about the mysterious processes taking place in the human body and for answers to some of the most profound unanswered questions in biology. As an example, consider the 2007 Nobel Prize in Physics, awarded for a quantum-based phenomenon known as giant magneto resistance (GMR).[2] There is a drive in the world of technology to make computers smaller and smaller. GMR made it possible to construct small hard drives capable of storing a terabyte (a thousand billion bytes) of data. To accomplish this, the hard disk had to have information very tightly packed as magnetic areas. A more densely packed hard disk requires a more sensitive read-out technique. The GMR effect accomplished this by using layers of metals only a few atoms thick. At the atomic level, matter behaves differently, exhibiting totally different material properties. Electrons have charge but they also have a quantum property called spin and GMR allows for information to be stored as electrons spinning in different directions.

All of this may seem a long way from biology but some biologists, and I am one of them, believe that the ultimate in miniaturization of physical phenomena has been accomplished through the evolutionary process that has led to humans. We will soon see that GMR technology is highly relevant to BodyTalk because it gives us a potential understanding of a special state of consciousness arising from the ways water molecules form microscopic molecular layers within the body. We shall see that this could be related to the way practitioners can interact with the fundamental processes by which both practitioner and patient are able to manifest health. But before discussing this some background is necessary.

While quantum physics is often regarded as the most important discovery in the history of science, biomedicine has been very slow to understand quantum phenomena well enough to apply the ideas to healthcare. Until BodyTalk!

In a way, the biologist and the astute therapist can study physics more easily than the physicist can. Biology and the healing process reveal physics in action in ways that can never be studied in a physics laboratory. BodyTalk is revealing quantum physics in action and is thereby telling us the truth about the subject in ways that are difficult to study in a physics laboratory and that are also difficult to refute. I have always thought that physics would advance in huge leaps if physicists would take a temporary break from the fascinating study of highly organized but thoroughly dead pure crystals and look at living crystals. This is why I personally appreciate biophysics, a field that encourages jumping back and forth between the biological and the physical perspectives on life. Biophysics is a rewarding field because it helps explain so many things that most of us are curious about. And this brings us to The BodyTalk System™.

I asked John Veltheim how he developed the system. His answer came as a surprise. I already knew that John had a long and distinguished career in Australia as a chiropractor, osteopath, and acupuncturist, and that he headed an acupuncture school in Brisbane for many years. I had assumed that BodyTalk emerged from his long and varied experience as a therapist. But the story goes much deeper. John explained that his real expertise was in philosophy, a study that began when he was a teenager exploring the martial arts and yogic scriptures. This led him to Zen philosophy, Taoism, and Advaita Vedanta.

John's career, like mine, turned around when he read two important books by Frijtof Capra: *The Tao of Physics*[3] and *The Turning Point*.[4] In these books, Capra documented how the founders of quantum physics struggled with the completely paradoxical world their laboratory experiments were revealing to them. In the end, they had to turn to the wisdom that had emerged long ago in the spiritual traditions with perspectives on the nature of reality and the role of Consciousness in the creation of the material world. Buddhist teachings provide rich descriptions of the connections between human Consciousness and natural phenomena. Notions of the interconnectedness of all phenomenon are described in many spiritual contexts. The concept is that there is one fundamental, universal substance that underlies all of life and the material world. The Dutch philosopher, Baruch de Spinoza (1632-1677), also taught that Consciousness and material phenomena are attributes of one underlying substance. Before quantum physics, there were no scientific methods available to study these ideas.

One of the leading interpreters of the Vedic scriptures, Adi Shankara, expounded the doctrine of Advaita, a nondualistic reality, in a famous statement:

"Brahman (the ultimate and universal origin and essence of all material phenomena, of all that exists) is the only truth, the world is an illusion, and there is ultimately no difference between Brahman and individual self."

As interpreted by Robert Lanza in his valuable book, *Biocentrism*[5], this means that: "What we believe to be reality is a process that involves our consciousness."

Our external and internal perceptions are inextricably intertwined. This is the aspect of quantum physics that led many of the founders of the field to the study of the Vedic scriptures. As they smashed atoms in an effort to find the fundamental "building block" of all matter, they began to realize that, if they could imagine a subatomic particle with particular properties, they would find a subatomic particle with those particular properties.

The behavior of subatomic particles – indeed of all particles and all objects – is inextricably linked to the presence of an observer (Heisenberg).

Without a conscious observer, objects exist in an undetermined state of probability waves (Schrödinger's wave functions). The patient in front of you has available a number of wave functions that can manifest health.

Scientists have discovered that the universe has a long list of traits that make it appear as if everything – from atoms to stars – was precisely tailor-made just for life to exist. The parameters describing the forces of nature are perfect for atomic interactions, the existence of atoms, planets, water, and life. Tweak any of them and we would not be here. If Planck's constant, h, were not $6.62606957 \times 10^{-34}$, the fine structure constant, α, could not be $7.297352533 \times 10^{-3}$ and we could not exist.

Time does not exist except as an animal-sense perception. Time is the process by which we perceive changes in the universe.

The very structure of the universe is explainable only through biocentrism: life creates the universe, not the other way around.

These biocentric concepts seem to be at variance with everything we have been taught about how the world works from the first days of our lives. However, biocentrism creates a powerful space for the conduct of BodyTalk. Biocentrism can also inform many other modalities in which Consciousness and intention play key roles. To be specific: empty space is not really empty. Empty space, combined with Consciousness, is a source of enormous creative wisdom and energy. It is the place from which all "things" emerge.

Distance is an illusion. We "see" objects as separate only because we have been conditioned and trained, through language and convention, to draw boundaries. Distance is not a useful concept when we are talking about "distant" healing. Many practitioners actually find it easier to treat a "distant" patient than a "local" patient.

Language about who we are treating, what we are treating, the names of diseases, the names of treatments, and how healthcare works or does not work are not useful in BodyTalk.

There are achievable states of Supramental intellect in which we have control over the manifestation process – choosing between different parallel possibilities or wave functions, both for ourselves and for those around us.

Inner coherence is one term that describes such Supramental states of Consciousness.

What do we mean by inner coherence and how does it relate to manifestation of particular pathways toward health for ourselves and for those we care about, both near and far? Is the Dirac Sea or Quantum Plenum the etheric space from which all physical manifestation emerges? How do we master these concepts?

Application of these discoveries to our understanding of human structure and function has been slow as images of the body as a machine composed of parts continue to dominate Western medicine. Great advances in molecular biology have led to an illusion that the most important questions in biology have been answered or soon will be. So impressive is the regularity, predictability, and reproducibility of chemical process that it seemed obvious to the molecular biologists that we would soon be able to understand how the entire plan of the organism is carried within the DNA and where the plan goes awry resulting in disease.

This optimistic point of view was expressed by James D. Watson, co-discoverer with Francis Crick of the double helical structure of DNA: "These successes (in understanding heredity) have created a firm belief that the current extension of our understanding of biological phenomena to the molecular level (molecular biology) will soon enable us to understand all the basic features of the living state." James D. Watson (1970).[6]

Vast sums of money, many careers, university departments, medical research institutes, and a giant pharmaceutical industry have been focused on finding ways to treat symptoms arising when the body fails to adjust, adapt, and repair itself. We continue to learn from these endeavors and many interesting ideas are being tested. However, the "master plan" for life and the actual cause of the major and most debilitating diseases have slipped through our fingers. How an organism develops into its adult form is a profoundly important, unanswered question. For the question also relates to how damaged tissue can be restored to its original form, and what goes wrong with this process in cancer and other diseases.

To solve challenging biological and medical problems, we must explore the basic aspects of life that mainstream biomedicine has traditionally been reluctant to examine. Viewed whole, the living organism displays properties that cannot be accounted for as a synthesis of the behaviors of parts. The problem is comparable to the unsuccessful efforts of physicists to find the fundamental building blocks of matter. We cannot find "whole systems" properties by taking things apart. Fortunately, holistic and systems thinking are becoming part of some academic trainings.

Those who have begun to provide a possible scientific basis for BodyTalk have not hesitated to explore topics that have been traditionally "off limits" to biomedicine. We owe much to them for their courage and willingness to go beyond the comfort zone of conventional thinking.

In a classic paper entitled "Contribution to the Whole (H)"[7], Andrew Packard, from the Stazione Zoologica Anton Dohrn in Naples, poses a vital question from his perspective as a physiologist working with squids: "How is it that an organism behaves as a whole, and not just a collection of parts?"

British biophysicist and Director of the Institute of Science in Society in London, Mae-Wan Ho, respond to Andrew's question from a quantum perspective: "Quantum physics provides us with an exact science for which a holistic view is only natural. It lets us understand how the wave functions of protons and electrons that make up an atom or molecule synch their individuality to a common wave function: an irreducible holistic property. I want to persuade you that a living organism is a quantum being, with a unified wave function, in the same way that an atom is."

Notice the use of the word "synch" in the above quotation. The term refers to a synchronization of quantum states that leads to quantum coherence, as will be described later in this Appendix. Notice also the concept that a living organism is a quantum being with a unified wave function. According to many standard textbooks in physics, quantum mechanics is a theory that is confined to the microscopic world. It works for particles, atoms, and molecules but is replaced by classical Newtonian physics on the scales of apples, people, and planets. This easy division of the world into small and large, microscopic and macroscopic is actually incorrect. Modern research shows that quantum principles apply at all scales, including molecules, cells, tissues, human bodies, and perhaps communities.[8] Quantum synch and quantum coherence may therefore be keys to understanding life and to understanding how BodyTalk works.

The term "holistic" has not been widely embraced by the biomedical community but there is a well-defined system within the human body that is particularly suitable for understanding unified or systemic effects including quantum leaps in health. It is called the living matrix. It is the only system in the body that touches all of the other systems. The more you understand the workings of this system, the more you will understand what is involved in being alive. The concept of the matrix came from the discovery that the fibrous network of the connective tissues, extending throughout the body, interconnects with the molecular fabrics within all cells (Figure 3). The key was the discovery of molecular complexes known as integrins that allow the extracellular and cellular matrices to form an interconnected continuum capable of transmitting energy and information forward and backward between cells and all of the connective tissues.

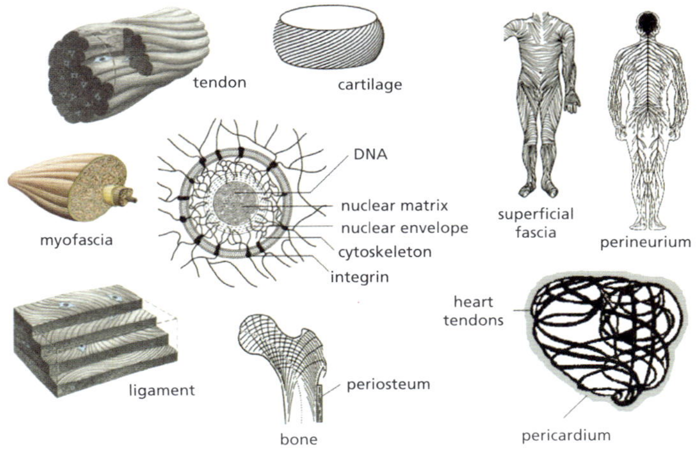

Figure 3: The living matrix.

When one includes all of the connective tissue systems shown in Figure 3, tendons, ligaments, myofascia, cartilage, bone, superficial fascia, the perineural system, the periosteum, and the coverings and linings of the compartments in organs such as the heart, it is apparent that we are dealing with the bulk of the living body. In terms of BodyTalk, the living matrix is an anatomically well-defined system in which we may find the unified wave function that approximates the whole person and the place to look for the inner coherence that leads to Supramental states of Consciousness. We shall soon see that new research is giving a clear picture of the nature of inner coherence. The living matrix is also proving to be a valuable interface between conventional or consensus science and the phenomena taking place in a wide range of other CAM therapies. For we know much about the molecular composition of the living matrix and about its systemic properties as a global regulatory network.[9]

During the 1980s, while the living matrix concept was being elucidated[10], the author's career took him into the world of Nobel Prize Winner Albert Szent-Györgyi and his colleagues at the Institute for Muscle Research in Woods Hole, Massachusetts. Szent-Györgyi had recognized that something profoundly important was missing from modern biomedicine and that this fact was greatly retarding progress in finding the causes of serious medical conditions such as cancer and heart disease. What was missing was an understanding of the movements of energy and information within the human body.

"Without energy life would be extinguished instantaneously, and the cellular fabric would collapse. The source of this energy is the sun's radiation." Albert Szent-Györgyi.[11]

The search for the something that was missing in medical science led Szent-Györgyi to the study of quantum physics and the quantum mechanisms involved in the movements of electrons in proteins and the structures made from proteins. Szent-Györgyi and his colleagues discovered that proteins are semi-conductors, materials with electrical conductivity intermediate between conductors, such as copper wires, and insulators such as plastic and rubber. Thus began a new field of science, which Szent-Györgyi called Submolecular Biology and Electronic Biology, the titles of books he wrote in 1960 and 1968, respectively.[12,13]

As often happens with new ideas, the semiconductor concept was immediately rejected by the scientific community. Experiments were done in which proteins were purified, dehydrated, squeezed into pellets, and placed between two electrodes. These samples would not conduct an electric current. Proteins are, therefore, insulators, or so they seemed, and therefore Szent-Györgyi was mistaken. However, there was a flaw in those studies. Water had been removed from the proteins. Without water, proteins are indeed insulators and essentially dead. If you study hydrated or wet proteins, you discover a very different picture.

The importance of Szent-Györgyi's seminal research was highlighted by microbiologist N.S. Hush of the University of Sydney in Australia in a 2003 overview of 50 years of progress in molecular electronics published in the Annals of the New York Academy of Sciences.[14] In his paper, Hush explained how Szent-Györgyi's fundamental insights have coalesced into "a thriving international research program in what might be called the ultimate nanotechnology." Hush is referring to the application of quantum physics in the design of molecular circuits that are fundamental to the development of the modern electronics and molecular electronics industries.

Electronic biology readily integrated with the living matrix concept, leading to the conclusion that the "circuits" involved in spontaneous remissions of serious diseases, as described by Andrew Weil in his book *Spontaneous Healing*[15] might provide a paradigm for an exact holistic science of the living organism as a quantum being sought by Mae-Wan Ho. This exact science might lead to an understanding of spontaneous healing and other quantum leaps in health, including those often observed in BodyTalk.

Modern research shows that water is not just important for semiconduction. It also contributes remarkable system-wide quantum properties. The reason for this is that the collagen molecules in the human body are very long and thin and many millions of them join in precisely spaced parallel arrays that can be viewed as giant organic liquid crystals (Figure 4a). Because of their regular spacing, these arrays yield sharp X-ray diffraction and nuclear magnetic resonance images showing that the amino acid components of the proteins are paced to make precise "perfect fits" for organizing chains of water molecules adjacent to them. H.J.C. Berendsen from Holland's University of Groningen first noticed this in 1962 using nuclear magnetic resonance.[16] Finally, because the water is so precisely organized around arrays of collagen strands, the water molecules themselves must be also regarded as a body-wide liquid crystalline system (Figure 4b). Further research shows that there are about three layers of water molecules surrounding each collagen strand (Figure 4c). These layers have the potential to develop phenomena similar to those produced by giant magneto resistance (GMR) described earlier. Applications of this phenomenon have revolutionized techniques for retrieving data from hard disks and for making magnetic sensors at the scale of individual spinning electrons. What is emerging is a completely new type of electronics known as spintronics. As a biologist, I suspect that life has taken advantage of such quantum phenomena and created memory systems that are far more sophisticated than a computer hard disk.

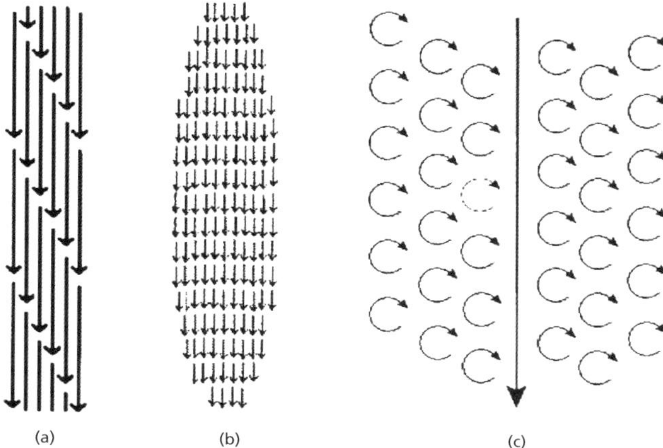

Figure 4

Recent research from the laboratory of Emilio Del Giudice and colleagues from the Instituto Nazionale di Fisica Nucleare (INFN) in Milano, Italy, and the International Institute of Biophysics (IIB) in Neuss, Germany, revealed profoundly important quantum effects and relationships in structures such as these.[17] These studies are not possible from the perspective of conventional quantum physics, but rely instead on discoveries in quantum electrodynamics or QED. One of the founding fathers of QED, Richard Feynman, has called it "the jewel of physics" for its extremely accurate predictions. Mae-Wan Ho has summarized the findings of the Italian physicists in a series of articles published in Science in Society, the periodical from her institute in London.[18]

The research shows that the water molecules associated so precisely around the collagen molecules form large quantum coherent domains. Here the word "domain" refers to a region characterized by a specific feature such as spin. Moreover, there is a tendency for vast numbers of spinning water molecules to synchronize their spins or to become quantum coherent (Figure 4c). It is important to point out that while water amounts to some 70% of the human body by weight, in terms of the numbers of molecules the body actually comprises 99% water. The other molecules, ions, DNA, amino acids, sugars, proteins and so on only add up to about 1% of the count. Among the exciting properties of such a system is the ability of coherent water domains to trap and store very weak electromagnetic signals from the environment (a possible basis for homeopathy) and a quantum-based mechanism for listening: "Sensory perception ... is the silken web that binds our separate nervous systems into the encompassing ecosystem." David Abram.[19]

When we think of sensory perception, we think of the so-called five senses, connected to the nervous system, that enable us to perceive what is happening in our local environment and also to sense what we are doing in that environment. This is the loop that enables us to see and influence the world around us, summarized with two words: sensation and action. The living matrix and its quantum properties provides for an entirely different system for sensing the environment and acting upon it, based on quantum coherence. As I have pointed out elsewhere[20], this system provides a possible basis for some of the remarkable phenomena taking place in cutting-edge athletic or artistic performances, in the martial arts, and in healing.

After watching BodyTalk in action, one begins to suspect that living matter has some extraordinary properties that encourage extraordinary healing phenomena. Mention has been made of inner coherence and Supramental states of Consciousness. The recent results from study of quantum coherence in the living matrix provide a possible window on such extraordinary transformational phenomena. This perspective results from the remarkable properties of water, identified by many investigators as the matrix of life itself.[21] When we talk about transformation, the biophysicist thinks of phase transitions,[22] such as when trillions of spinning water molecules in the living matrix, shown in Figure 4c, come into synch, creating quantum coherence. The most familiar example of phase transitions are the changes water undergoes when ice melts and liquid water turns to steam. A tiny shift in temperature produces a virtually magical transition. These transitions are a kind of amplification, with a subtle change in temperature leading to a radical change in material properties. Such phenomena are pervasive in biology and play a central role in the drama of life.

What is emerging is an understanding of a quantum system that simultaneously entangles every part of the body of the therapist and every part of the body of the patient. It is a system capable of a definable and understandable type of shift in coherence that allows for a unified wave function and a palpable shift in Consciousness. Some will argue that this is total speculation and it absolutely is. For this inquirer, a speculative explanation is better than no explanation because it provides something that can be confirmed or refuted.

For a fascinating account of entanglement, see *The Age of Entanglement* by Louisa Gilder.[23] For a critique of entanglement, see a 2010 report by Christian.[24] For a discussion of the idea that the universe is alive, see a remarkable book by Duane Elgin.[25]

To conclude, quantum physics and BodyTalk are providing possible explanations for a new way of viewing health. The phenomena observed in BodyTalk support the quantum view, and the quantum perspective described as biocentrism (Lanza) supports BodyTalk. These discoveries are transformational to say the least. These concepts come at a time when many are looking to science and medicine as a way to transform global consciousness and lay a foundation for a new Golden Age. Again, Szent-Györgyi has a message for us in his fascinating discussion of syntropy, or the drive in nature to perfect itself.[26] His captivating article on this subject is a discussion of the relationships between the biological and physical sciences. Szent-Györgyi lists a number of biological phenomena that cannot be explained without considering that the universe is alive and has a fundamental property that provides an actual drive or evolutionary tendency toward improvements – toward higher levels of order. The idea is that there is a fundamental wisdom hidden below the visible surface of the natural world that pushes evolution in a positive direction. It is the same wisdom that has driven matter to generate life and to build up life's mechanisms.

In essence, Szent-Györgyi is discussing the ancient concept of Brahman (the ultimate and universal origin and essence of all material phenomena, of all that exists) as described in the most ancient of the Buddhist texts. For these ideas, Szent-Györgyi was reproached for being a vitalist, mysticist, obscurist, and teleologist. I do not worry about such names, as I follow the advice of Will Rogers: "Why not go out on a limb? That's where the fruit is."

In the end, though, what we do with all of this is up to us. Stated differently: "Whether you think you can, or whether you think you can't, you're right." Henry Ford

References

1. Planck M. On the Law of Distribution of Energy in the Normal Spectrum. *Annalen der Physik.* 1901;4:553

2. The 2007 Noble Prize in Physics - Press Release. Nobleprize.org. http://www.nobelprize.org/nobel_prizes/physics/laureates/2007/press.html. Accessed November 6th, 2012.

3. Capra F. *The Tao of Physics: An Exploration of the Parallels between Modern Physics and Eastern Mysticism.* 5th ed. Boston, MA:Shambhala; 2010.

4. Capra F. *The Turning Point: Science, Society, and the Rising Culture.* New York, NY: Bantam; 1984.

5. Lanza R, Berman B. *Biocentrism: How Life and Consciousness are the Keys to Understanding the True Nature of the Universe.* Dallas TX: Benbella Books; 2009.

6. Watson JD. *Molecular Biology of the Gene.* 2nd ed. New York, NY: W.A. Benjamin Inc; 1970.

7. Packard A. Contribution to the Whole (H). Can squids show us anything that we did not know already? *Biol. Phil.* 2006;21:189-211.

8. Vedral V. Living in a Quantum World. Quantum mechanics is not just about teeny particles. It applies to things of all sizes: birds, plants, maybe even people. *Scientific America.* June 2011:38-43.

9. Pischinger A. *The Extracellular Matrix and Ground Regulation: Basics for a Holistic Biological Medicine.* Berkeley, CA: North Atlantic Books; 2007.

10. Oschman JL. Structure and Properties of Ground Substances. *American Zoologist.* 1984; 24:199-215.

11. Szent-Györgyi A. Oxidation, Energy Transfer, and Vitamins. A Nobel Lecture. Nobel Lectures in Physiology or Medicine 1922-1941. Singapore:World Scientific Publishing; 1937.

12. Szent-Györgyi A. *Introduction to Submolecular Biology.* New York, NY: Academic Press; 1960.

13. Szent-Györgyi A. *Bioelectronics.* New York, NY: Academic Press; 1968.

14. Hush NS. An Overview of the First Half-Century of Molecular Electronics. *Annals of the New York Academy of Sciences.* 2003; 1006:1-20.

15. Weil A. *Spontaneous Healing: How to discover and embrace your body's natural ability to maintain and heal itself.* New York, NY: Ballantine Books; 2000.

16. Berendsen HJC. *Nuclear Magnetic Resonance Study of Collagen Hydration*. J. Chem. Phys. 1937;36:3297-3305.

17. Del Giudice E, Tedeschi A. *Water and the Autocatalysis in Living Matter*. Electromag. Biol. Med. 2009;28(1):46-52.

18. Ho M-W. Coherent Water and Life. Science in Society. ISIS Report July 22, 2011;51:26-29. Ho M-W. Quantum Coherent Water, Non-thermal EMF Effects and Homeopathy. Science in Society. ISIS Report July 22nd, 2011; 51:30-33; and a series of earlier articles in the same journal.

19. Abram D. *The Spell of the Sensuous: Perceptions and language in a more-than-human world.* New York, NY: Vintage; 1997.

20. Oschman JL. *Energy Medicine in Therapeutics and Human Performance*. London, ENG: Butterworth Heinemann, Elsevier; 2003.

21. Collins JC. *The Matrix of Life*. East Greenbush, NY: Molecular Presentations; 1991.

22. Pollack GH, Chin W-C. *Phase Transition in Cell Biology*. New York, NY: Springer; 2010.

23. Gilder, L. *The Age of Entanglement: When quantum physics was reborn*. New York, NY: Vintage; 2008.

24. Christian J. Disproof of Bell's Theorem by Clifford Algebra Valued Local Variables. Cornell University Library. http://arxiv.org/abs/quant-ph/0703179. Updated April 22nd, 2010. Accessed November 5th, 2012.

25. Elgin D. *The Living Universe: Where are we? Where are we going?* San Francisco, CA: Berrett-Koehler Publishers; 2009.

26. Szent-Györgyi A. *Drive in Living Matter to Perfect Itself.* Synthesis. 1974;14-26.

Appendix B
How to Do the Cortices Technique

Here is the Cortices technique, explained in detail. Feel free to experiment with it to see its effectiveness for yourself. The Cortices technique, besides being the first one that practitioners learn in BodyTalk, also forms part of a set of five basic techniques, known collectively as Access, which can be learned in a day and practised daily on oneself and one's family with great results in maintaining health.

Firstly, all BodyTalk techniques – including the BodyTalk Access techniques – rely on a tapping process to bring them into effect. The light tapping over the head is used to activate communication in the brain and then the light tapping over the sternum stores the memory of the changes that are being made. The tapping process involves spreading the fingers to reach over both hemispheres of the brain and gently tapping on the head. This alternates with the fingers lightly tapping over the center of the chest on the sternum to activate the energic heart complex. The scientific theory behind the technique has already been covered in Chapter 5.

How to Tap

Tapping of the head is accomplished by spreading the fingers and thumb so that both hemispheres are contacted across the midline of the skull. Tapping of the heart is done over the center of the chest on the sternum, or breastbone, with the focus on the heart underneath. All tapping is done lightly at a comfortable speed. Since the focus is on the movement of energy to create a standing wave, the tapping will still work even if the head or chest is not physically contacted at all. This is a consideration in areas of the world where it is culturally inappropriate to touch someone or even illegal to touch another person for therapeutic purposes.

The tapping is alternated between the head and heart. It is not necessary to synchronize the tapping with the breathing. Note that it is possible to access the heart energy not only by tapping on the sternum but, if it is more convenient, by tapping on the back in between the shoulder blades. The heart's energy pattern is accessible from both sides!

Throughout this technique your focus is on connecting all points of the right hemisphere of the brain to the left hemisphere, so as to draw the blood supply to all parts of the brain. This will eliminate any "cold spots" of diminished blood supply or reduced cellular activity so that your whole brain will be able to function more effectively in an integrated way.

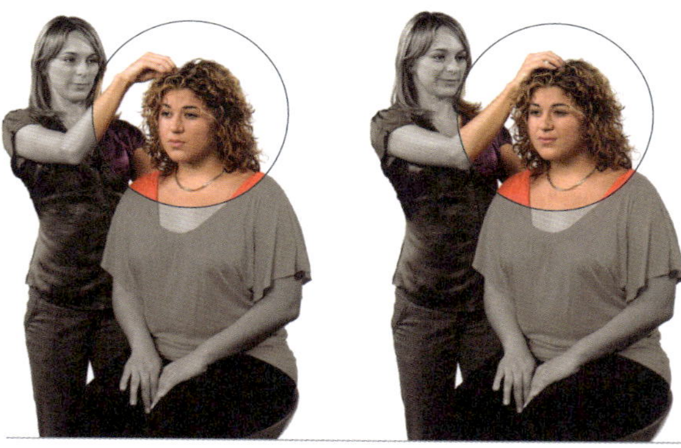

Incorrect Tapping: Make sure both left and right hemispheres of the brain are contacted

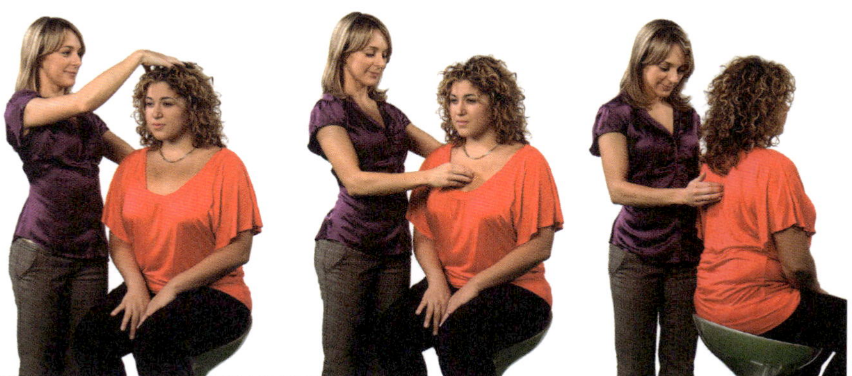

Correct: Fingers spanning across both hemispheres of the brain

Tapping the sternum

Tapping the back

The Cortices Technique: With A Partner

Place one hand on the person's head at the base of the skull where it meets the neck. (Note: It is important to keep the fingers and thumb together throughout this technique to avoid missing any areas of the brain.) While holding that position, use your other hand to tap the head and then the sternum (or back) lightly, alternating between them for two full breath cycles of deep breathing.

Now move your hand up the head to the position next to the one you just used. (You are going to systematically cover the whole head, one hand width at a time.) In the new position, tap out the head and sternum, again alternating for two full breaths.

This procedure is repeated until you have covered the whole midline of the head from the base of the skull to just above the eyebrows. This could mean three hand widths for a large hand to cover a smaller head or five hand widths for a small hand to cover a larger head. The main objective is to make sure that the entire head is covered. The hand positions may overlap to ensure that no areas are left untouched.

Now cover the sides of the head to balance the temporal lobes. Preferably, have the person cover both sides of his or her head with their own hands. Or you can cover both sides of their head with your hands for a few seconds. Now tap out while the person takes two full breaths. (If you are doing it the second way, let go with one of your hands to tap the head and sternum [or the back] then reverse hands.)

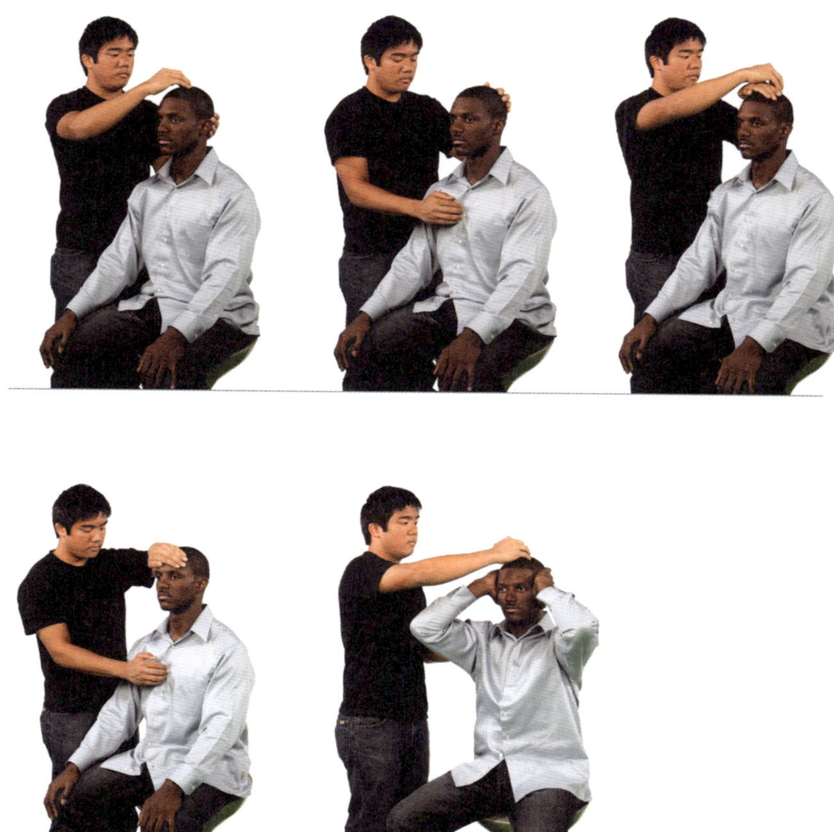

The Cortices Technique: Self-Application

Place one hand, with fingers together, at the base of your skull, so that it straddles both sides of your head and covers the top of the neck and the bottom of the skull. While holding this position, tap the head and then the sternum with your other hand, alternating for two full breath cycles.

Now move your hand up onto your head just above the position you just held. (You are going to systematically cover the whole head one hand width at a time.) In the new position, tap out your head and sternum, alternating for two full breaths.

Repeat this procedure until you have covered the whole midline of the head from the base of your skull to just above your eyebrows, making sure that the entire head is covered. Your hand positions may overlap to ensure that no areas are left untouched.

Now cover the sides of your head to balance the temporal lobes of your brain. After holding both sides of your head for a few seconds, let go with one hand and while still holding one side of your head, use your other hand to tap on your head and then on your sternum. After each head and sternum tapping, place your tapping hand back onto the side of your head for a few seconds. Now hold the other side of your head while you tap over the head and sternum. Continue this process for at least two full breath cycles of deep breathing.

Benefits of Using the Cortices Technique Regularly

With regular application of this Cortices technique, you will find that your head may feel less “foggy,” your mental focus may sharpen, or you may just feel more balanced and clear. Try it out. You can do no harm and the process has the potential to do so much good.

Maximum results will be experienced if you start out using the technique every day as a routine. It only takes about one minute to perform and you should get into the habit of doing it regularly, for example after you have brushed your teeth. After a week you will start noticing improvement in many aspects of your health and wellbeing. After a few months you may find that your inner stress levels have normalized for the first time in your life!

Appendix C
Advanced Case Studies

Sandra

Symptom profile

Sandra is in her mid-40s and in the past two years has been experiencing major digestive disorders. She feels bloated after eating and doesn't feel like she's digesting her food properly. If Sandra doesn't eat on time or misses a meal, she goes through classic "sugar swings" involving mood changes and depression. There is a family history of diabetes and her doctor, through blood testing, considers her to be pre-diabetic. Sandra is also clinically overweight and chronically tired.

BodyTalk session

My hand is on her upper abdomen and I am feeling the aortic pulse while intuitively observing the heart function. The heart is laboring and there's evidence of a very slight murmur. This is a very common occurrence caused by a variety of stress factors relating to the heart energy system. There is a slight rotation of the heart within the chest cavity. I am using the Body Vivaxis technique to correct the heart's position. Effecting this correction means that the heart-brain complex can effectively store all the changes made throughout the session so that the treatment will have a lasting effect.

I am now drawn to the liver, which needs a general correction to restore full function. A CDRRII is being utilized. The defrag component of the CDRRII is specifically targeting the Krebs cycle of the liver in order to normalize fat metabolism. The coordination matrix for the Krebs cycle has been compromised over many years so that it now needs a defrag of that function in order for it to work normally from now on.

I am now at the pancreas, which has a build-up of epigenetic markers that are gradually changing pancreatic function. Active memory issues starting in early childhood have caused unhealthy activation of five of the markers. I'm picking up that during early childhood, the parents were going through major financial concerns coupled with disharmony in their relationship. As a young child, Sandra was very stressed by her home environment. This stress situation and her experience of it caused Sandra to adopt a set of negative belief patterns and assumptions. The impact of childhood environmental stressors and deeply ingrained, learned assumptions about life resulted in a personality that will always attract worrying situations in her life process. This theme of stress and worry dictated a lot of her social interactions throughout her life, giving rise to a long thread of active memories. These are being addressed by running multiple Active Memory techniques in a dynamic recursive formula to neutralize the stress factors maintaining the epigenetic markers. The body will then break down the epigenetic markers thereby changing the function of the pancreas.

Another set of four epigenetic markers was caused by chemical damage starting in fetal life. The main trend here was that the mother was smoking heavily during the pregnancy and many of the chemicals found their way into the embryonic fluid giving the baby a toxic environment. This smoky environment continued throughout her childhood because of the heavy smoking by both parents. The Body Chemistry technique is now clearing the toxic build up in the system which will then neutralize the epigenetic markers.

There are two epigenetic markers that I would call the "seed" markers. They are so named because they are the hereditary markers that would ensure a thread of stress factors throughout her life would lead to diabetes. I am going back to the hereditary factors on her mother's side. I am now at the great-great-grandfather who suffered from quite extreme occupational heavy metal poisoning. I am now addressing the morphogenic energy field (a 64 tetrahedron) holding this information in Universal Consciousness. Multiple Body Chemistry dynamic recursive techniques are correcting the stresses held in these energy fields. When completed, this will result in the two hereditary epigenetic markers being dissolved.

A general CDRRII formula is now running in the pancreas in order to restore its normal function. The pancreas needs to re-contextualize and re-evaluate all its functions relating to the digestive system. There will be particular emphasis on a defrag of the coordination matrixes related to the production of pancreatic enzymes and insulin.

I am now linking the liver, pancreas, and adrenals in order to re-contextualize and re-evaluate their functional relationships. This poor relationship was a major factor in Sandra's energy levels because the adrenals were malfunctioning.

Feedback

I talked to Sandra six months after the BodyTalk session and she explained that it took about 10 days for her digestive system to normalize and she has remained symptom free for the following six months.

Jim

Symptom profile

Jim presented as a 52-year-old successful businessman who had been in quite a severe depression for five years. He was very concerned about his brain function because he could not think clearly, had poor memory, and got confused easily. He was also getting chest pains after any form of exercise. Medical testing of his heart showed there were some blockages occurring in the arteries and veins due to a build-up of cholesterol and he was told that he would soon need bypass surgery.

BodyTalk session

I am first drawn to the heart and liver and concur with the diagnosis of cholesterol build up particularly in the heart. I also see that the circulation in his brain is being compromised by a similar build up that would make him vulnerable to a stroke. I'm now running a CDRRII on the liver function to restore the normal breakdown of fats in the system. I'm also running a Fragmentation program on the cholesterol lining the walls of the blood vessels in the heart and brain. This will clear the blood vessels within a few days. I see there is already some degeneration of a small patch of heart muscle in the left ventricle because of diminished blood supply. Therefore, I am running a Rehab program to regenerate that tissue. (The Rehab program is another advanced formula using PaRama BodyTalk, which can regenerate tissue in specific locations.)

Now I am focusing on the brain and see that Jim has many lesions in the brain. Head trauma or high stress levels usually cause these. Although these brain lesions are small, they pose a major problem for people as they get older because they interrupt the neurological functioning of the brain. Jim verified that he has had several hard blows to the head causing concussion. The blows caused minor vascular accidents that brought about the formation of these small lesions. I am now running a Circulation Plug-in to the brain along with a Fragmentation program to systematically break up the lesions and clear them. This will make a very big difference in total brain function within a few days.

I am now drawn to the thalamus, particularly section 8 of the thalamus, which is involved with organization and planning. This section is connected internally to the liver meridian function. It is interesting to note that the liver function (Consciousness) concerns the planning and organization of many of the main biochemical functions of the body. Jim confirmed that he is quite a heavy drinker. The alcohol damage to the liver has, through the liver meridian, affected the function of section 8 of the thalamus, leading to his general confusion and inability to plan and organize his thought processes.

I am now doing a CDRRII on the liver meridian to correct its function. This will, in turn, correct functioning of both the liver and the thalamus. Parallel to the CDRRII, I am running a Body Chemistry formula to correct sugar metabolism. Jim's Innate Wisdom has clearly indicated that he has a strong allergic reaction to sugar which in turn is a major contributing factor in his drinking problem. The correction of the sugar allergy in conjunction with the improved brain function should bring to an end his tendency to drink excessively.

Feedback

Six weeks later, Jim reported that he felt as if he had an entirely new brain. His thinking was clearer than it had ever been, even when he was young. He was starting slowly in an exercise program and there were no chest pains. Four months later, I received an e-mail from Jim to say that his heart specialist was mystified by how healthy his heart now was.